TWO
LESSONS
OF JESUS

GREGG TOMUSKO

TWO LESSONS OF JESUS

JESUS NEVER SAID THAT!

TATE PUBLISHING
AND ENTERPRISES, LLC

Published by Tate Publishing & Enterprises, LLC
127 E. Trade Center Terrace | Mustang, Oklahoma 73064 USA
1.888.361.9473 | www.tatepublishing.com

Tate Publishing is committed to excellence in the publishing industry. The company reflects the philosophy established by the founders, based on Psalm 68:11,
"The Lord gave the word and great was the company of those who published it."

Book design copyright © 2015 by Tate Publishing, LLC. All rights reserved.
Cover design by Jeffrey Doblados
Interior design by Gram Telen

Published in the United States of America

ISBN: 978-1-68118-591-0
Religion / Christian Life / General
15.07.14

Contents

Part I

God

1

God's Religion Is Beautiful

He taught that we are spiritual sons and daughters of a loving Father.

He left us the example of his life, from birth to after death.

"God is spirit," Jesus revealed. Jesus handed us eternal truths.

He said God is a father. He said God is His father. He said God is our father.

Jesus became man to reveal our spiritual Father. His good news: we too are spiritual sons and daughters of God.

The only prayer he gave us, the Our Father, reaffirms this lesson. Some do not get past these first two words. The impact shoots through their minds and hearts, like two electrodes in a blast furnace that, with a blinding flash, melts steel, and they cry.

That knowledge should change our lives. Our dad—yesterday, today, and through eternity—happens to be the sovereign God of the Universe.

Jesus showed what the Father, if in the flesh, would be like. Jesus revealed God to man by becoming a man. Does the Father have a personality? How does he act?

The answer: Jesus. "If you know me, you know the Father." To the complex problem of getting to know God, even intimately, He gave us Jesus. To show that he cares deeply, God became Jesus.

Jesus left us an example of how to live a life on earth when you know you are a beloved son in a family ruled by love.

The majority of his life was ordinary, like ours.

Jesus lived life as a human. As a human, he figured out how his Father wanted him to handle every situation and then handled it in that way.

Do as I do, befits Jesus.

Since even if the heavens and earth pass away Jesus's words remain, do as I do and as I say, befit Jesus.

He left no possessions, perhaps for fear we would worship objects.

He left nothing written, perhaps for fear that his followers would offer a book rather than speak enthusiastically about his life.

Jesus knew he would resurrect himself and be able to talk to each person on earth who desires his presence. Spirit can be omnipresent. He explained the advantage of leaving his mortal body where he could be in only one place. His spirit could be with all men for all time at any place.

Jesus wanted to speak special words to each of us, a personal message from one who knows us and loves us and has lived as one of us. When we think about his life, Jesus promised to stand before us, look into our eyes, and then to update and personalize his words in today's setting and specific to our lives.

The teaching of Jesus: accept God as our Father.

Spend some time to talk to our Dad. That's all he asks of us.

When we have a baby, we become a mom or dad. We share with God creation and being a parent.

What hopes do we have for our precious babies?

God asks the same question.

All the good we desire for our children originates from God our Father.

Conclusion

God the Father wanted His relationship with us to be that of father to son or father to daughter. So His holy, infinite Spirit came down to dwell in our minds. He placed the key to the kingdom of God right in our grasp.

To an evolved animal—one with a decent brain, but still an animal—God offers divinity. An alchemist changing granite to gold seems a puerile parlor trick by comparison.

To become a swimmer, we must get in the water. To become divine, we need knowledge. To be told we are a son of God, we need faith to believe it, and we need to respond, to act as would a son of God.

Our best relationships form deep roots of love. God longs to have this relationship with all His children and at all times. Of all the ways we've tried to rule others, God rules his universe by love.

2

God Forgives Any and Every Sin We've Committed

Accept divine forgiveness. Nothing beats being forgiven. Nothing compares to coming home.

We need to have nothing between us and God.

If purity can be achieved on earth, it occurred on my first Communion. All sins forgiven, Jesus blessed me and stayed in my heart that whole day. Friends and relations were happy for me and showered me with smiles and gifts.

After the ceremony, I walked by our spring flowers in front of the house. The colors were bolder and brighter than normal. I got a sense that there was an unseen world being shown to me.

From that time, when I sinned, it weighed heavily. It seemed nothing could go right. My thoughts became paralyzed, and I froze, cautious to stay alive until I could find the first opportunity to go to confession. I experienced great joy and comfort when forgiven.

This has to be a foundation to a religion: to be forgiven by God. St. Peter would have been miserable and useless if he had not been forgiven.

No one brought this home more than Kierkegaard. He explained there are no ifs, ands, or buts. We are forgiven, period. To worry about anything after this "meeting with eternity" constitutes despair. The sin of despair questions forgiveness, hoping to tap into a lack of faith. Do not worry about anything; God washed and purified our soul's slate board with ammonia until squeaky clean.

All sin can be forgiven. If we are in rebellion against goodness and consciously choose sin as a way of life, we would no longer desire to be forgiven. Such a mind degrades until no longer normal, to the point where even though forgiveness patiently waits for the person to return, they keep walking farther away, soon passing the Very Difficult and, finally, the Impossible to Return signpost.

They will to not be forgiven and so debilitate until no longer capable of sincere repentance. Jesus referred to this state as sin against the Holy Spirit. The existentialists named it nothingness. The physicists explain that all things tend toward entropy. If we resolve to walk off a cliff and go one step too far, we cannot undo the fall. When we reject God's plan to be his child, we die spiritually, which also cannot be undone.

There is sin. There are devils. There is nonsurvival. And there is forgiveness.

Accept divine forgiveness. Reconcile with your family so you no longer feel estranged and can again fully enjoy their friendly company and love, and please our Father.

Of course, kids disobey their parents. Kierkegaard figures, "Thank God for the distance between!"

Good parents always love their children. Only we, the child, can reject that love.

Conclusion

Ask for forgiveness. It's the only way we'll feel good about ourselves, and to make sure we're invited to the next party!

Part II

Transition: God to Man

3

God's Religion Is Beautiful, Man's Less So

God's religion exudes beauty.
    Spiritual truth flows freely from it.
    The living truth soars like a butterfly.
    Some look and admire.
    Some want to know more, and seek.
    Some use tools, and dissect.
    Some want it dead.

Quite often, by the time someone presents the butterfly to us, it expired in formaldehyde with a pin stuck through its thorax, and except for a short description someone scribbled, we can only imagine it flying.

Jesus wished he had more time with his apostles because they were slow of understanding. He had so much more to tell them. He has more to tell us.

Jesus carefully evaded getting immersed in the affairs of his generation and concentrated on teaching man to live as a son of God. His life two thousand years ago remains relevant today. Though times change, he continues to teach unchanging truths and to make them personal and understandable in each of our own life experiences.

We enjoy Jesus's Spirit of Truth, a "real, living, breathing" person, Jesus minus a human body. The word *breathing* in this context means "life-giving." At Pentecost, Jesus breathed upon those in the upper chamber, and every man and woman on earth possessing an open heart received this new life. This Spirit still breathes over the earth.

Jesus's spirit comes personally to us, ever available to help us get through each day if we want the advice of God. We cannot see him, but we can certainly feel his presence when our hearts burn within or when we see something clearly for the first time or when we somehow know without a doubt that what we're hearing resonates deep down as true. Our experience on this planet gets us closer to heaven, provided we make good choices. Experience serves us as a wise teacher.

Maybe "it's a lousy experience because we're lousy people." Perhaps a bit nonelegant, but it does succeed in getting a point across: in the universe, not only are we the lowest, at the very bottom of the chart of will-creatures, but also our peculiar history left us spiritually challenged. Having our major spiritual leaders—Lucifer and then Adam and Eve—screw up puts us about a million years behind. We are confused, rebellious, disobedient, and many would like to kill God. Our planet needed a visit from God. Those who take this visit to heart enter a better world, a kingdom of heaven while still here on earth.

Man tries his best to understand God, and religion evolved from sacrificing the most advanced man and woman of a tribe to convince the moon to shine (during a new moon) due to a paralyzing fear of darkness, to the affection and love many enjoy with God today.

Relationships are real, and loving ones last. Relationships happen with persons and not a church's set of doctrine.

For the sake of unity, we tolerate other's well-thought-out understandings, even if different from ours. The apostles all had their own interpretations of Jesus's parables and the meaning of his life. They shared a love for Jesus and a desire to help others in the way they thought Jesus counseled.

If they didn't always get it right, why do we assume we do? We certainly try our best, and will someday graduate from kindergarten! In endless time, in eternity, we will learn something new every day about God that we did not know before.

We preserve what we believe reflect God's teachings in what we call religion. We do not suspect that the warning of the man who buried the talent—to return the understanding of Jesus as comprehended two thousand years ago—applies to our religion. Why give a gift of truth at Pentecost to the entire world when we knew it all back then?

Man's religion often looks like a butterfly in formaldehyde. Jesus wants our spirit free, to fly.

I taught algebra to ninth graders who couldn't multiply; they were not ready for algebra.

Jesus honestly assessed his apostles: "For so long I've been with you, and you still don't understand."

Jesus taught spiritual truths.

After some two thousand years, Jesus only needs to change names and date: "So long I've been with you, and you still don't understand."

We are not that far along spiritually.

Conclusion

God taught we are sons or daughters. Forgiveness follows. To have meaning in our life, we must live out this lesson.

Whatever man touches gets altered, normally for the worse. We need to always go back to basics: if it doesn't derive from sonship, we introduce error.

Part III

Man

4

Jesus Did Not Come to Earth so Sins Can Be Forgiven. Jesus Never Said That

St. Paul first connected the death of Jesus with the forgiveness of sins. Jesus never said this. This idea originated with St. Paul.

St. Paul had a personal experience with the risen Jesus. Before that, he persecuted Jesus.

I assume Paul prayed to know the truth, and then the only way Jesus could get through reduced to throwing him off his horse and blinding him. Otherwise, why not convert every nonbeliever in this same way?

Paul saw the truth that Jesus was alive and God, and wanted to serve him.

Paul did not enjoy the personal experience of sitting down and talking to Jesus in the flesh. He did not hear the teachings from his mouth or enjoy the physical presence of Jesus as man. St. Peter and others who lived with Jesus disagreed with Paul's interpretation of the words and life of Jesus. This belonged to Paul as his own personal response and understanding of Jesus. It was spirit filled but not entirely correct.

Jesus made no connection between his horrible death and the forgiveness of sins.

Jesus taught that there exists no greater love than laying down one's life for others.

Jesus willingly laid down his life for others. Jesus chose to leave heaven to become his lowest creation: man. Jesus faced the struggle to make a living and experienced sad occasions and death. When he was fourteen his father died, he submitted to Roman authority, faced being unable to buy enough food, and endured a painful death—all because he wanted to show man that God loved them. His only concern during his horrible passion focused on the safety of his friends. He laid down his life for others, for us. He lived as one of us, which was the Father's will. He showed through his life and words God loves us. All this we believe true. Jesus never made reference to a sordid deal he made with his Father that unless he dies a horrible death, God the Father won't forgive anyone's sins.

If Jesus's plan to win over the Pharisees to embrace his renovations to religion succeeded, Jesus would have died a natural death and been more successful.

Jesus lived his entire life for others and died for others. Jesus's end-of-life provided a remarkable example of a human facing death, and dying. If we talked to Jesus or Lazarus after they died and are now alive in the flesh, it would bring home Jesus calling himself "the resurrection and the life." Jesus showed us how to live and how to die and promised his friends life after death.

So why, in over two thousand years, did no one question that Jesus died to obtain the forgiveness of sins? My mother would ask, "Where'd you get a crazy idea like that?"

Nietzsche stands as the first. He wrote a book called *The Antichrist*, where *anti* here means that the way we interpret Jesus's life little resembles what Jesus taught or lived.

I naturally rejected Nietzsche's thinking, encountering it as a teen. I struggled, still grasping the fact that not everyone fills in "Roman Catholic" under religion, let alone challenge a fundamental belief. Nietzsche's unique thinking enthralled me, just the fact that someone would think it!

After years of exploring other thinking, I find I agree with Nietzsche. Only one question leaps to the top: "Is this true?" That forever reigns as the key question.

Paul's Motivation

The Jews rejected Jesus. They made no connection of this man with the teachings in the Old Testament. How can Paul convince the Jews when he had the same mind-set his entire life?

Paul naturally wanted to win over his fellow Jews, especially the ones like him who persecuted Christians.

Paul had a brilliant idea: Jesus became a sacrifice, the last sacrifice ever required. He fully appeased God. In a flash of genius, he hit upon the only possible way to convince tradition-loving Jews that Jesus did match the prophecies. Accept Jesus as a sacrificial lamb—right from the Old Testament—who appeased God, once and for all time, for our sins.

We no longer require the slaughter of animals on the altar. Jesus's sacrifice totally restored the favor of God upon his Jewish people.

Even the Pharisees did not murder Jesus but sacrificed him.

Evolution of Religion: The Importance of Sacrifice

Since food proved essential to the lives of primitive man, they set apart and worshipped some of the larger animals. Early man drew pictures of these big creatures on stone. When the venerated beast died, they performed worship services around its carcass. Later in man's evolvement, he sacrificed these animals as an act of worship. The idea continued down to Moses, who identified acceptable sacrifices. Paul finalized this doctrine of the "shedding of blood" to obtain God's renewed favor.

Early man feared God. God needed blood to grant favors: to prevent volcanoes from erupting and to provide food. It took until the time of Moses to end human sacrifices among civilized people. Moses gave rules for animal sacrifices acceptable to God.

When the Jews sacrificed an animal to God, they believed that God dwelled in the animal as they consumed it. Eating became a religious experience.

Animal sacrifices ended with Paul. Jesus pleased God, fulfilling the role of the last sacrifice needed.

We equate blood with life. A heart pumping betokens health. We give blood to saves lives. Doctors bled persons with "bad" blood, believing it would save them.

To sacrifice our son on the altar constitutes the ultimate act of faith in God. Abraham willingly agreed to do so and became known as the father of faith.

Blood plays an important role in science and religion.

Our knowledge continues to expand. At least, we're supposed to be getting smarter.

We no longer bleed people, but we look at their blood for clues as to what disease they have. Some researchers trace unsolved cancer to parasites, or something irregular in the blood. If in the blood, it can latch on anywhere, and cancer appears everywhere. Cancer may be in the blood.

However, we don't kill our own sons to prove our faith. But we still believe God the Father did.

Even the Old Testament author has God saying "Of course don't kill your own son! I'm testing to see the limits of your faith. It has no limits." That's the point of the story: a faith with no bounds.

In our interpretation of the New Testament, we have God willing to sacrifice his own child. This God not only goes through with it, it's premeditated.

This won't fly for the role of a loving God who wants to be known affectionately as Dad.

This caused confusion for centuries to thinking men and women. Kierkegaard reasoned that it lies beyond human understanding and crosses over into the absurd. So faith must be the acceptance of the absurd. Nietzsche simply described it as being wrong, that we interpreted this badly. Jesus was murdered.

Man's Thinking

Like hard-hearted businessmen, we ask, "God, what have you done for me? What have you done for me lately?"

I repeat my learned response: "I sacrificed my life for yours so you would not spend eternity suffering in hell." It's hard to find a better answer. It's clear what's in it for me: a future payoff. That future—our death—often seems a long way off.

What about now? From my experience, I'd answer (for God): "I let you live how you want to. I offer no special favors. You might get a terrible disease and suffer for years and then die alone. You may not have enough money to feed your family. You could become a prisoner and be tortured by the enemy." He's pretty much a hands-off manager, not sure of what he does.

To think that we were not under a death sentence and Jesus did not come here to be brutally murdered so I could have my death sentence revoked hits hard and is tough to give up. Many love Jesus because he suffered for our good. He saved us.

Jesus came to show us how to live and ended up brutally murdered. We're the barbarians. We're the murderers. Not God. Not in God's plan.

Every father understands the following. Our son goes off to war for the good of others. He is killed. The father cries, heartbroken. The mother stares blankly through tears, devastated. Both understand why their son went and understand the country stands better for him going. That equates to what God the Father also understood.

No father understands this: within our enemy's borders, citizens kill each other, take drugs, get drunk, cuss, and teach hate propaganda against our nation.

Our leader seethes and will only forgive the behavior of our enemy if he sends his son to be killed by these people. Furthermore, the killing has to be vicious.

Not a very good solution; not sound thinking on the part of our leader.

We have the same analogy in Christianity. Many don't analyze God's thinking and are content that our sins can be forgiven and that we can achieve happiness in the next life. Kierkegaard offers that this must be divine logic that lies beyond man's grasp. Nietzsche named it foul logic.

Nietzsche shines as the first to see this in a new light.

Jesus taught man how to live as to be godlike, and ugly man murdered this innocent and beautiful person. Man must be mad. How can he not be overwhelmed with pity? Nietzsche's goal became to help man by teaching him how not to pity, to face the deed he did and then make something better of ourselves. Become a son of God by behaving like one.

I think Nietzsche comes as the closest to understanding Jesus.

His book *The Antichrist* challenged my thinking, once I got over the title. I knew he thought a lot about the life and words of Jesus. I don't know if personally he was a spiritual person. Since the mind serves as the gateway to spiritual treasures, he certainly kept that door wide open.

He may have precociously detected that man tends toward being an—and then becomes more—antichrist. He forced men to take a long look at what they did: they brutally murdered a good and innocent man. Knowing we're capable of that, Nietzsche asks how we're going to change and believed that Jesus answers that question.

Am I Screwed if I Do the Will of God the Father?

The Father's will directs us to love one another. He wishes the best for us. We wish the best for our children.

He wanted his son to be greatly loved by everyone on earth and to live a very happy, long, and productive life.

Cruelty cannot exist in God and remains totally foreign to him, never a part of his plans. Cruelty results from the absence of good, and God contains 100 percent goodness.

Cruelty may infect the will of some men who hurt others. Jesus never promised to pull us out of the way of hurtful men. He did promise he would go through every ordeal with us. He knows what it's like to go through bad times, having gone through them himself.

As long as bad men breathe, we may be screwed if we do the will of God the Father. These men hate God, hate Christ, and hate Christians. Doing the right thing often gets men killed. It will be that way until "thy will be done, on earth as it is in heaven."

We fulfill God's will when we love one another. In heaven, there is zero tolerance toward sin. On earth, we are so twisted as to think tolerance reveals how good of a person we are.

I didn't always keep my earthly parents in mind, especially while experimenting in adolescence and asserting independence as a young adult. After experiencing raising a family, I not only appreciate my parents more but also am amazed at how they were able to give us so much with so little.

I never questioned my membership in my family. I can't imagine what I would have to do to lose my parents' love; never wanted to. I think no matter what, they'd always want the best for me.

I never asked their forgiveness. When I did something thoughtless, I'd argue and realize I stood in the wrong. Forgiveness followed, often unspoken. I wanted to get back to the way things were and made every effort to regain their confidence.

Conclusion

The entire theology of Jesus suffering so that our sins can be forgiven falls flat and presents an unreal view of the Father—indeed, of any father.

St. Paul's salesmanship to win the Jews by employing the Old Testament approach that we can offer a sacrifice to please a god wrought with the human emotion of being greatly offended by our transgressions sets us down the wrong path.

Nothing good can be found in murder. Blood contains no magic power or any spiritual worth.

Faith no longer centers on the suffering of Jesus but highlights how he faced this tragic act of man.

5

God Works in Natural Ways

Jesus did not plan to perform miracles.

God came to earth as a man, not as God of the universe.

Jesus decided that he would live and then die as all men must. He would not take advantage of being God to help himself out of any unpleasant situation.

As he began his ministry, he went up on a mountain to pray and seek spiritual guidance, to try to figure out what would please his Father. Jesus decided he was to reveal his Father, and do so as an ordinary man. That was what the Father wanted. He would not use miracles to win over the people. Nor would he fulfill the Old Testament prophecies of a conquering king. He would live his life working out problems using his human mind and not his divine mind.

Perhaps this was his thinking.

What's the best way to show man and woman that I love them?

I will become a man, and love them.

What's the best way to show man and woman how to live on earth?

I will become a man and live a life on earth.

Jesus figured that if he's to experience life on earth and to teach men about God, he needs to do it as a man. And so God became man. Otherwise I can just hear "Sure, it's easy when you have supernatural powers. Try surviving down here with no powers." He probably heard me.

Jesus decided the following: "I will not use my divine powers for myself. I could create all my food, but I will labor for it. I could make my life easy, but I will earn my leisure time. I could prevent accidents and keep myself safe, but I will not circumvent physical laws. I could prevent any disease, but I will try to keep my body healthy and face sickness, old age, the breakdown of the body and mind, or anything else humans face. I could end my incarnation and avoid death, but others don't have that option. I will even experience death. No matter what, I will live and eventually die as all humans have to."

God lived an ordinary life as a man, even a common man.

He did not become part of the intellectual class. He worked with his hands.

He did not use eloquent speeches. He spoke simply, using natural comparisons.

He did not intend to start a religion, let alone become its leader. Until near the end, he spoke little about himself and always about his Father.

As a man, he figured out what God had willed for him to do and become.

He quickly came to understand that he was also God. He had an existence before being born on earth.

What was the Father's will? For Jesus, it was to lead men to personally know God as a father.

If Jesus lived only as a human who demonstrated faith in God, and in so doing revealed God's father-to-son relationship, then Jesus accomplished the Father's plan. No proof of Jesus actually being God changes a man, and so he planned to offer none. He did not even intend on telling anyone he was God.

Jesus went alone for forty days to develop plan A: to live a spiritual life here on earth as a human. Submit the human will to the divine will. Learn to attempt communication with God, with the spiritual fragment of the Heavenly Father within all of us. Teach about God. Teach the teachers. Hope that the Pharisees embrace his newer and more spiritual understanding of the scriptures.

His approach concentrated on winning over the Jewish leaders by teaching them that they are sons of God. Hope that by faith they grasp this truth. Hope that this truth will change them so that they actually behave as one whose father is God. Hope that they teach this truth.

It didn't work on the religious leaders. Who would imagine that the ones most knowledgeable of God on earth would reject God's teachings? They were the greatest chance of anyone in the whole world to embrace this truth, yet they would not leave the security of theology and face the fear of what a new spirituality would do to their lives. We face the same challenge today.

Jesus had to forget the Old Testament. He will not fit the prophecy. None of them fit him. The only Old

Testament description that came close to describing him he gleaned from the book of Enoch, speaking of a man of peace, a "son of man"—a title he adopted.

The Old Testament prophets did not clearly foresee Jesus. The Jews, who spent every evening in study of the scriptures, saw no connection of Jesus with the promised Messiah. It should have been obvious if the Old Testament's Messiah described God. Instead, they asked, "Aren't you the carpenter's son?" Those with advanced degrees in the scriptures, similar to today's doctorate, were insulted that unlearned common folk referred to Jesus as the Messiah. The Pharisees were infuriated, and later ready to put him to death when he then went further and called himself the Son of God.

Jesus spent considerable time with his apostles dispelling their concepts of the believed promises of God to his people Israel.

The prophets spoke of a warrior, a leader of the Jews who would overpower the Romans, expel the conquerors, and reign as king. That wonderful promise hardened like concrete in most Jews' minds and so ingrained in Jesus's apostles' thinking it blocked any conflicting idea. They continually asked, "Is now the time? How about now? I've brought my sword. Can I be your number one commander? Can I be on your right?" They repeatedly asked him until the time they saw him hanging on the cross.

The Jewish leaders would have to put aside this hope of self-rule in order to fulfill a more spiritual role.

Except for a handful of times when Jesus became so moved by compassion or someone's faith, Jesus's daily routine resembled ours. God, who could do anything, chose to not use his divine powers the vast majority of the time. Jesus never did and never will attract spiritually mature followers by miracles. His attractiveness rested on how he lived his life, not on his ability to perform miracles.

He refused to use his supernatural powers for any gain, let alone to kill the Romans. Jesus knew no lasting attraction to spiritual things takes place in people looking for shortcuts, unfair advantages, or special status. They soon learn that God does not show favoritism.

The only way to win over another consists in an appeal to the spirit that resides in the mind of man. This time-tested spiritual approach survives as the only approach Jesus used, and will ever use, and the technique he taught his apostles.

He places us in the middle while he communes with his Father's spirit dwelling in our minds, as if we pick up the phone and listen in on a local call.

When Peter realized that Jesus was God, Jesus explained, "This knowledge was not given to you by man but by my Father's indwelling spirit."

If I had supernatural powers, I would use them. Do you think I would work? You think I'd have someone telling me what to do? You think I'd let anyone put me to death? I sure wouldn't share my ability with others. I'd never lose my advantage of power. I'd only help me and avoid any danger to myself.

Jesus didn't.

Why Did Jesus Perform Any Miracles?

Jesus chose to live as a human. Humans don't perform miracles.

Jesus certainly performed miracles.

God being physically present on earth inevitably would result in supernatural events.

Jesus, being both human and God, to live only as a human, proved not an easy task. Jesus had a divine mind and a human mind and did not have an off switch for either. In his divine mind, time did not exist. God views all time in the present. Time lives only in his human mind as a succession of events. An event that would take humans a month, Jesus could accomplish instantaneously. Without time, something started, worked on for years, and then completed happens in the same instant. From water, grapes, and added ingredients, grapes ripen, ferment, and become fine wine over time—instantaneous for God. While philosophically sound, such explanations of reality outdistance my grasp. For Christmas, I need a better mind!

God possesses unlimited creative powers. Anything the Son wills in harmony with what the Father wills is. That desire comes to be.

The human mind of Jesus wished the wedding couple brought enough wine. The compassionate human heart of Jesus willed the large crowd of sick and crippled healed. Since the Father willed the same, it happened.

The combination of an infinitely compassionate heart being present among us moved Jesus on several occasions to use his miraculous powers. Maybe someone's faith touched him deeply and he cured their ill. Jesus put into effect very limited use of his power and instructed the recipient to tell no man.

Jesus—being God—exuded spiritual, uplifting, healing, joyous, positive energy, and being in the flesh comprised a one-of-a kind occurrence. When the woman with the hemorrhage touched him, he felt energy leaving him. To avoid any superstition, Jesus made it clear that the woman's living faith enabled her to tap into his healing power—now resident in his physical presence—and not from the cloak he wore.

Despite instructing otherwise, his apostles still clung to the old prophecy of a warrior king. If the ruler had miraculous powers too, so much the better. All the Jews judged him against this vision.

Jesus used the multiplication of the loaves and fishes to teach his apostles he will never fill the role of a temporary king. He appealed to the multitude by feeding them without having to work; he performed a miracle. They were won over and declared Jesus their king. A few days later, these same five thousand shouted, "Crucify him!" Jesus hoped to teach his apostles a valuable lesson. Will his apostles see enticing men through miracles lasts as long as a meal of loaves and fishes? Will his apostles work to transform people in a more permanent manner using spiritual methods?

As a last-ditch effort, Jesus completely changed his tactics. He boldly stated that he was God. He performed several miracles to challenge the religious leaders' hardness of heart. The Jews were rejecting him and his teaching. "If I brought a man back to life, would they still not believe?"

Jesus resorted to plan B: Admit that he is the Son of God. Challenge the rulers as a last-ditch effort for them to admit that raising the dead cannot be penciled in under Everyday Occurrences. Maybe we should listen to him. He now presented himself as the Son of Man and the Son of God. He upbraided the Pharisees for their blindness and slavery when they steadfastly rejected him and continued to adhere to what they were taught.

In many ways, Jesus's plan failed. The greatest teachers of the time certainly weren't going to spread his new ideas. Most followers vanished. His closest companions hid, devastated and holding little hope.

Jesus cried out, "My God, My God, why hast thou forsaken me?" and shortly after died.

Jesus sounded devastated too, with little hope even in God. I've heard many good explanations, but none seemed quite right. Jesus never felt forsaken by God.

Then I ran across this: Jesus recited scripture for comfort when dying. Some passages were overheard. It took me a long time to find this explanation, and I believe it true.

Fortunately, what man cannot accomplish, even God as man, God can. Jesus resurrected himself. Jesus poured out his Spirit of Truth over mankind. The apostles made tremendous spiritual progress in a very short time after being empowered at Pentecost and transformed this world.

Men recorded the miracles of Jesus. They skipped over the 90 percent of quiet labor in everyday living.

Jesus has full power to heal everyone. Jesus has full power to make earth a paradise. He possesses miraculous powers. Do not expect a miraculous change. Expect day-by-day learning and us making better decisions.

We are not attracted to Jesus because he performs miracles. We are attracted to Jesus because he *is* a miracle. It takes a miracle for God to become man. Metaphysics deems it impossible. We cannot grasp something infinite compacted into something finite, let alone actually becoming his lowest free-willed creation.

What Separates Christians Is the Miraculous

How much supernatural power did God entrust to humans?

Here we differ. Jesus never demanded uniformity of thought, but he did demand unity. For Christians to be so divided makes him cry. "A house divided against itself will not stand" describes his house. Christianity can no longer afford to be split. There can be found a greater good than hearing "Yes, you were the only one that was right."

Which no one will hear. Our understanding of religion still evolves. Our minds slowly expand, ever learning more about the art of living.

Churches sincerely try to understand the Word of God in the Bible and to account for traditions with hopefully sound origins. Certainly we rely on the presence of Jesus's Spirit of Truth and the leading of the light of the Holy Spirit as we try to understand.

We progressed as far as the enlightenment of our times has taken us so far.

I don't suppose any of us will get very far on this assignment: construct an eye.

The being next to me in class made an eye having vision in about a half of a second and felt insulted he received an assignment so puerile. I don't know where to even begin. We need a little humility. We think humans always get it right when we rarely do. We bring incompetence to the table. The expression "I'm often wrong but never in doubt" fits.

We often share the same goals. Here lies the key to unity. We can disagree on doctrine. St. Peter certainly disagreed with St. Paul, and both were great Christians.

How much power did Jesus leave his apostles?

"Peter, you are rock, and upon this rock I will build my kingdom."

Or did Jesus say, "Peter, my Father's spirit in you is rock, and upon this rock, I will build my kingdom"?

Jesus knew people would desire to worship together, so he provided leadership in the church. The church formed as the social manifestation of hearing the good news of Jesus. Every organization needs a hierarchy to maintain order.

Christians agree that the divine power comes from God. The Holy Spirit gives life to the church. As to whether the Holy Spirit or man decided each Church's doctrine, we differ.

I think if I told St. Peter of his infallibility on certain matters, he would laugh at the thought and then shed tears, remembering being unnerved by a servant girl. St. Peter preached some profound truths that certainly did not come from being a professional fisherman. Yet he never claimed to be infallible.

People needed dogma and definite answers. They needed a rock to anchor their beliefs in. The church provides this, provided that when the church drops the anchor, it sails deep into the cleansing waters of the Holy Spirit.

I've observed the definition of *church* change from an emphasis of a holy building with a tabernacle where the priest says Mass to now being centered on the people who attend. In catechism class, now called Public School Religion, we defined *church* as a holy place run by a holy priest, and we could see our church structure best when viewed from outside. Today, the emphasis centers on the holiness of the people. St. Paul called the people the body of Christ, the visible presence of Christ on earth and capable of providing physical and spiritual aid.

I think the meaning of *church* will remain "a holy people." The fragment of God the Father that dwells in each of our minds compares well to a solid foundation, the rock that Jesus spoke to Peter about.

We will naturally want to share our happiness and worship together. Since every social organization needs a hierarchy of widening responsibilities, Jesus placed Peter as head to maintain worthy membership and provide leadership.

Jesus preferred to worship outdoors. We have beautiful gardens and parks where we can worship. We also have beautiful churches, well maintained by a dedicated group of volunteers motivated in serving others, where we can worship.

When I thought I was going to be drafted to Vietnam and either killed or tortured and then thrown in a cage, I wondered how I could remain Christian if I did not go to Mass and receive Holy Communion. That's when I concluded that church means something more spiritual and less ecclesiastical.

I advocate going to church. I believe I can have a close relationship with God by praising him while in a national park. I believe I can communicate with Jesus and the Heavenly Father anytime I contemplate his life. But I'm lazy. If I'm not forced to go to church, before long, days and weeks go by without me even thinking about God. I don't like being forced through the threat of mortal sin. I think this approach to promote the good shall eventually take on a more positive form. When we do look back, we must recall that the church's motive to coerce people to spend time with God proved fruitful, and God judges by our motives. Sadly, if I don't have to do something, I won't do it. The underlying impetus of fear worked as a blessing for me.

If I spend no time with God, I toy with spiritual death. A checked-off list of evasions proves more deadly than a mortal wound. Cancerous black spots of sin soon darken the x-ray of my soul.

"I will give my flesh for the life of the world."
How can you give us your flesh?
"My flesh is real food, and my blood is real drink."

(Note: The conversation continues on the next page and read as next week's gospel.)

It is the spirit that gives life. The body is of no value.

The above can also be stated in this manner:

"I will give my flesh for the life of the world. My flesh is real food, and my blood is real drink."

How can you give us your flesh?

It is the spirit that gives life. The body is of no value.

When was the question about giving actual flesh asked? Which answer did Jesus give?

The early Christians celebrated Jesus's last supper as a fraternal meal where they remember and reflect about the things Jesus said and did here on earth. They recall that he was once physically present among us.

In doing so, we become more as one as Jesus enters our heart and communes with the Father's spirit that dwells within each mind, and we participate in this three-way reunion. Our soul shines and grows through this intimate moment with God akin to a father hugging his returning son and placing a diamond in with his son's belongings.

We become vicariously the two brothers on the road to Emmaus. Our hearts burn as we listen to the words of Jesus. When we break bread, we recognize Jesus still present with us and open our hearts to his love.

Our spiritual eyes can discern his presence as we feel him enter our heart. Jesus promised to be here for each of us since the day he poured his very own Spirit of Truth over the entire earth—Jesus minus his physical body—to always be with us, anywhere, anytime. He established a common occurrence—eating—so we remember to commune with him at least three times a day.

The Jews slaughtered a lamb in honor of God; they believed they received God when they ate the meal. Christians recall the Last Supper, and the food becomes spiritual food: Jesus himself fully present in body, soul, and divinity.

Which body—physical flesh—resurrected "new form" or spirit since "God is spirit"? The theologian within cannot help but to step forward and preach!

The literal interpretation of the food actually becoming human body and blood—transubstantiation, the Catholic Church teaches. I would not want to be a missionary in Africa explaining that we eat human flesh under a different appearance. And we are not cannibals.

Some modify this to being Jesus's resurrected body, composed of chemical elements, but not human flesh. If you combine "This is my body, this is my blood" with the empty tomb, we conclude Jesus materializes physically present in the Eucharist in the postmortal form. We conjecture that the body's chemicals reformed in the new resurrected body, especially given this body appeared as visible to human eyes. We cannot see spirit or sup with a ghost.

"Remember man that thou art dust, and unto dust though shalt return" seems consistent.

Dust, though useless, could provide chemical building blocks of our resurrected body.

Jesus states that the body has no value. Physical elements don't help one's spiritual life but, like scaffolding, forms a temporary bridge from our world to the next. God consists of spirit, not physical elements. So even if we receive things of the earth, that part has no spiritual value. Only the spiritual presence of Jesus matters. We grow spiritually based on the spiritual reality that we can love and be loved by God and feel united with Jesus in a deep relationship, deeper and more permanent than marriage. Only physical things seem real to us, and only spiritual things as real to God. The physical we touch, feel, taste, and can hit our heads on, God views as shadows cast by the spiritual.

I happened on this explanation of the empty tomb: Jesus's body did return to dust. The angels requested that it decompose naturally but without time or instantaneously. Angels, horrified at how we treated our loving creator, hoped to avoid watching his body decompose.

As an added bonus, I can finally apply something from my Freshman Cosmology class: time does not exist. What happens over years can still happen; the change just took zero time.

Our postdeath body contains both still-physical and spiritual components, but the dust remains in the tomb. A metaphysical substance not found in our periodic chart provides the raw material of our resurrected body and our soul. It can be made visible to human eyes but subsists indifferent to matter. Jesus experienced the life of a human both on earth and after death, so he took on this newly resurrected body that we also will be given. Jesus experienced being a man both alive on earth and alive immediately after. This explains why he asked Mary to not touch him as he was not as he was here in the flesh and why he would appear and then vanish before wondering eyes.

Still, God is spirit. So even this quasiphysical body lasts a short time and then shed once Jesus returned to "the right hand of the Father" as the human-experienced ruler of the universe.

The scriptures state the body has no value. So we are not teaching physical flesh or metaphysical substance but spirit. Jesus makes himself present, as himself, as spirit.

We all agree on Jesus's presence at Communion.

The disagreement reduces to the definition of his "body."

I'm not even going into the idea that the Almighty God, being pure spirit, would not require a soul. Man needs a soul to survive. We have need of a spiritual part from God to partner with. God does not need a soul to survive. He always was and always will be.

Jesus stands before us, "body, soul, and divinity." Jesus physically present means being truly present. Let's not dissect him or argue over the word *physically*.

After death, sitting at a meal with Jesus and experiencing his tremendous love for us and feel so close and safe that our eyes go moist from joy, we will live in spiritual communion with him and little care how it's done. Jesus is truly present.

Why This Comparison?

Why did Jesus say "This is my body" if he knew we will take his words exactly as spoken?

Perhaps Jesus figured we would not take his words literally; we would never interpret this to mean eating his physical body. His teachings concern spiritual realities. How do you explain spiritual realities to a creature?

Jesus also spoke about the "kingdom of heaven." Jesus did not like the term *kingdom*, which then implies a king. He used the expression, and almost every Jew knew that meant kicking some Roman butt! They took him literally.

"This is my body" initiates a spiritual event. Two people embrace; one is God, the other man. Two personalities commune—relate to one another, feel concern and love, enjoy one's company, refresh each other, laugh, fraternize in fellowship. We walk away feeling more loved, spiritually strengthened, and desire to know more about God and be more like God.

Perhaps Jesus referred to his body, his physical presence among us; a man among men. I am God on earth, right here before you. Many will desire to have had been here with me, as you are.

"Take notes! If you listen to my teaching and follow me, you will live. I am the bread of life. I am the truth, the way, and the life. Without me you can do nothing." Jesus, a humble person, simply stating the way things are.

Why bread and not meat loaf? Bread satisfies a basic need for survival. Jesus called himself the bread of life: without a desire to know Jesus, we will not survive. Without the basics, we starve.

Jesus built on the Old Testament passage where God sent down bread from heaven for his people. Jesus offers more from God, the living bread sent down from heaven, here among his people. Eating physical bread does not help spiritually: their fathers died—permanently. If you consume Jesus, are so taken up by his life that you begin to think like him and act like him, you will never die spiritually.

Why wine and not water? Wine has qualities to uplift our spirits, help us forget our daily cares, to help us relax and enjoy good conversation, and appreciate each other's company.

When I was in the seminary, there was a debate on whether to put a beer tap in our gathering place. Our English teacher noted that "some of the best conversations I ever had were over a bottle of beer." That clinched it for me.

Perhaps Jesus would explain: "I am here to quench your spiritual thirst. Blood running through my veins gives me physical life. My entering your hearts gives you spiritual life."

We stop to eat and drink throughout the day. Stop and remember me and the life I lived here among you. Envision that someday you will sit at my supper table. Let the bread and wine remind you of me. I am here with you now.

His meaning may be more simple and natural than we've made it. Simple things are often the most profound.

Why Is Transubstantiation so Important?

If the host (bread) does not change into the sacrificed body of Christ, it would lead to the thought that Christ did not die so that my sins can be forgiven.

He sacrificed his body on the cross as payment of the terrible deeds that man did and continues to do against God. Man's sins keep Christ on the cross, eternally suffering for love of us. He gave his body for the life of the world. He saved us. He took our sins upon himself and took on all the suffering that they cause and accepted their just punishment. Without this sacrifice, sin would not be forgiven.

He then established the Last Supper, giving us his body and blood under the form of bread and wine to strengthen us from sinning by receiving him—body, soul, and divinity—into our very selves. We become more like him the more we receive him.

The Catholic Church deems these fundamental beliefs.

Holy people have given up their lives rather than change one word as written. This belief turns ordinary men into heroes in life, selfless souls dedicating their lives to others, powered by a deep love for Jesus. Simple lives turn sublime by faith.

There are those who receive the stigmata or have witnessed flesh and blood present in the host.

I believed this most of my life. I know it draws people closer to Jesus. It also takes joy out of some lives and turns some away from the attraction of living a life as Christ lived.

Christianity Is Depressing: Sin, Sacrifice, Guilt

Here are some conclusions that seem to fall out from these beliefs:

God intrinsically linked love to suffering. For proof of how much Jesus loves us, we look at his torture on the cross for our sins.

God approves of the innocent suffering for the guilty. Jesus, an innocent man, murdered for our offenses.

A loving relationship with God could only be established through a human/divine sacrifice. Because Jesus suffered and died on the cross, our sins can now be forgiven.

Jesus's physical body and blood possesses spiritual value; flesh saves us. We relive his sacrifice on the cross during Mass, and his physical body appears, taking the form of bread and wine.

The priest has "divine" powers. He consecrates the host (the bread and wine becomes the body and blood of Christ) and has power to forgive or not forgive a penitent. Through a priest, we reconcile with God by going to confession, where we admit our errors and obtain God's forgiveness through "divine" power given to a priest.

God holds one's progeny responsible for the sin of an ancestor. Our relationship with God ended because of the fall of Adam and Eve. Through the power of the priest at baptism, he removes our original sin.

God plans people's death. The plan for Jesus centered on his acceptance of a horrible death. Even today, when a child dies, we explain the tragedy as God's will.

If we follow the will of God, we choose a death sentence. For Jesus, the will of God meant his suffering and death. If I submit to follow God's will, something terrible will happen to me.

We remain in constant need of repentance. We always displease God.

How much of this can be traced back to earlier concepts as religion evolved on earth, and how many reveal eternal truths? How many resulted because our religion evolved just this far, and a thousand years from now, we will look back and wonder how we ever believed such a thing?

Let's take a look way back from today.

Families, united by blood ties, later united with others to form tribes in order to survive. It was first the custom to kill all strangers, later to enslave them, and still later to be adopted into a tribe that began with a ceremony of drinking each other's blood. Early man then diluted the blood with red wine and afterward drank the wine alone. To seal the ceremony, they clinked glasses, drank the wine, and feasted.

In early peace traditions, they would cut their skin then suck each other's blood.

As a lad, the idea dawned to become blood brothers, or real close friends. The procedure commenced with taking out our pocket knives—which we all carried—cutting our finger, and mixing our blood with another's blood. I'm not sure anyone did this because no one wanted to cut their own finger, but the concept ranked as cool.

The efficacy of blood became ingrained in our evolution. Many of our beliefs tumbled out of theological discussions.

We need to know that Jesus's Spirit of Truth remains here on earth to help us discern truth from partial or completely erroneous deceits and to talk to us about his

Father in heaven. Citing the authority of the church as an excuse to not think about these matters only appeals to an indolent and nonprogressive soul. When we shut off thinking encouraged by the Spirit of Truth, we are telling Jesus to shut up! The unquestioned authority of the church fails to attract those looking for the truth and bread of life.

The shaman maintained the most powerful position of the tribe since they believed he possessed spiritual powers. Nietzsche's criticism of "priests holding on to power" because they allow their flock to believe that they have been granted powers given by God becomes clear if viewed as a continuation of these early days.

What if every one of these beliefs turns out to be the thinking of man and not God? The CSI team dusting for fingerprints on the murdered Jesus found "man" working alone. What if we trace all this back to man's interpretation and God never implied any of these beliefs? What if the responsibility of stopping Christianity from blossoming falls on each of us, as Nietzsche proposed? What if we built stone-walled churches to keep Christ out?

We prefer the butterfly under the glass. I think more doctrine originates from the thinking of man than God.

Jesus Expects Christian Unity

Realizing that those who do not believe exactly as we do are still good Christians helps us achieve unity.

My daughter had a friend in school and played over at her house. One week later, the family vanished. They had received a call to serve Christ in Africa and uprooted their children, possessions, all. They did not belong to my church, but I suspect I know who the greater Christian is.

"Quo vadis?" Some ask only this question. St. Peter departed from Rome because of Christian persecution. When he saw the Lord, he asked, "Which way?" (*Quo vadis* in Latin). The Lord directed him to Rome to comfort the Christians. Without hesitation, he headed back and helped his fellow Christians. Nero crucified Peter on a cross, upside down as per Peter's request as he did not feel worthy to die the same way as Jesus.

With God as our dad, loyalty belongs to our Father in heaven. We siblings must maintain a strong and unified family. You go to the church you're comfortable with, and I'll go to mine. But if someone attacks our Father, we join forces.

Does Science Disprove Religion?

Science proves that God follows the physical laws of science that he established in biology, chemistry, and physics.

When we look at a single cell and witness a million chemical formulas working perfectly for the well-being of the whole, we call it impressive but not a miracle. If I list all million chemical equations to accomplish this and conclude God does not exist, I may be very intelligent but not very smart; I lack wisdom. The conclusion does not follow from the facts.

When we can wait nine hundred billion years from the initiation of the Andronover nebulae to the formation of a single planet that could sustain life and God views this as occurring "in the blink of an eye," we see God working in natural ways takes time.

God utilizes the laws of science that he established in his toolkit.

We're impressed when a college professor fills up three blackboards. Imagine filling up every blackboard in the world to evince the best chemical equation to produce a biologic reaction to replace an injured cell with a healthy cell and then running half a million scientific experiments to discern the best design for a cell to heal a wound. We should not deem this intelligent design but as very intelligent design.

The big bang theory deserves high marks. From a huge explosion, a bright star sits surrounded by circling masses, one of which lands the exact distance from the sun to one day support human life. One mile closer, and humans burn up; one mile farther, and humans freeze. Through bombardment of meteors and multitudinous geologic changes, land mass slowly forms. Lava and incoming meteors use up all the available oxygen. Plants were then needed to be designed to take in the sun and expel oxygen in order to achieve a breathable atmosphere.

From an implantation of genetic material into a few ponds on earth, life develops and modifies, adapting quickly for survival. Genetic combinations and mutations produce unusual and varied offspring. Whole species survive. Whole species cease to exist. "Big and dumb" turns out to be a bad combination. Huge dinosaurs eat all their food supply and starve. The brains and swiftness of the more progressive mammals begin to dominate.

Hostile geologic changes sometimes eliminate almost all life on a continent except for a few survivors in one locale. Then conditions again change and allow them to migrate.

Life nears extinction, often localized. The description of Noah's ark, where a great flood destroyed life except what Noah saved on his ark, provides a good illustration of earth undergoing huge geologic changes where a majority of life was wiped out, leaving only a small pocket in a single area to carry on evolution.

When a superior evolvement appeared, the inferior may exist for only a very short time. Finding intermediate species with a brief span of existence borders on the near impossible. There may be no fossils.

A planned benefit of extinction: today's oil.

Evolution helps solve the puzzle. From lemurs, a sudden mutation produces a being capable of decision: man. Limited resources and sharing hunting grounds lead to survival of key traits—and wars. As in all wars, we witness the elimination of some key traits and the survival of less desirable traits. A retarded couple in the lineage of early man hid during one devastating war where few survived. When war was over, they came out of hiding and headed south to warmer climes. These became the parents of our modern chimpanzees and other apes.

Through science, our designers achieved a life-sustaining planet inhabited by a creature with will—the human—and a wide variety of animals with capable instincts to survive. We now live on a planet with unique and diverse animal and plant life. By allowing experimentation, certain advancements were achieved in the science of life design.

In an ensuing geologic age, a twenty-thousand-foot-deep glacier covers most of the earth, advancing into North America as far down as present-day Kansas.

After the Ice Age, we had freshwater lakes with drinkable water in large bowls.

Early red man killed off all mastodons, just like later blue (white) man killed the bison. Food stayed scarce. Survival remained difficult, which forced man to be creative and inventive just to survive.

Man grew more intelligent as the result of harsh survival conditions.

Science does not disprove God. Science proves that God works in a natural way. God obeys and utilizes the scientific laws that he established.

Evolution continues, always purposeful and never accidental. Preplanned and well-thought-out by what we might call a supergenius, for lack of a better word, or to imply God had a hand in it, which he did.

Why Is God's Creation Not Perfect?

Take gravity, a physical energy created by God and controlled by God throughout the universe. Earth's gravity functions perfectly. It works every time. Everything else seems a little screwed up. A physicist would remind us, "All things tend toward entropy." A grobian, "All things turn to poop!"

We make plans, and they go wrong, some literally up in smoke. If you've ever worked out a flawless project plan and then watch others totally screw it up, you've experienced things not going as planned.

A drawing I find humorous first sketches a swing with a tire hanging from a tree branch by two ropes and titled *What I Asked For*. Next we see a tire taken prisoner and tied tightly to the trunk, labeled *What We Got*.

If the project really goes south, the owner of the company may come and do what he can to repair the damage, but it will take a herculean effort to fix everything. Needless to say, the project's end date extends way into the future.

That describes earth's spiritual history. God's plan versus what actually happened.

The theory that all things evolve bumps into contradictions. We discover a reversion of primitive plant life to the prechlorophyll level of parasitic bacteria, which now cause our death. Some snakes reverted from land due to overcrowding and returned to the sea. If man embraces sin, the basic drives of prehistoric males rule, and we become more like an animal.

God is perfect. God created heaven as perfect. That little blue-green ball living on the outskirts of the universe looks troubled. Earth cannot be so imperfect unless God delegated this project to someone else. I bet the "kids" are to blame.

For us, God's kids makes up a very small family. We have three pictures on our mantle: God, angels, man. God displays what looks like a million pictures crowding his huge mantle and covering his walls. He shows off photos of the many diverse beings that help run his vast universe. He planned for and created many different orders, with varying degrees of divinity and perfection.

God had divine but imperfect sons design all the life on our planet. Many of their experiments and modifications turned out very successful. Employing biologic evolution, before the last combinations and mutations of genetic material reached completion, a creature with a will successfully evolved. Little could these designers predict what a different course we would take from almost all other planets in thousands upon thousands of local universes like our own. It is very, very rare for a son of God of a very high order of near-perfect beings to go astray. But ours did. Lucifer declared war on God. He left such a mess that Adam and Eve couldn't take it and defaulted.

The "kids" are at fault. We blame their parents: God.

Since I'm such a miserable curmudgeon, I'll give God the bad review: the dreaded Needs Improvement. Here I present my list of his mistakes, where I felt forced to give him low marks:

- Using evolution to create man. An instant creation results in a better specimen and takes way less time.

- Using experience as a means to make the lessons stick. I keep doing the same stupid things a hundred times and still don't get it. I acquire common sense immediately after someone tells me the answer. Like a magic trick, once someone reveals the secret, the problem seems trivial. Till then, I've exhausted everything I could think of. So just show me all the answers, and then I'll get it. The other way, experience, doesn't work for me.

- Putting Lucifer in charge of earth. You knew he was falling in love with his own brilliant personality and mind, and you can see the future. Pull him before he really screws up and takes all of us with him. With one race, one language, and the survival and procreation of only the best traits in humans, brotherhood would be a reality.

- Letting Adam and Eve, who were sent to uplift the races culturally and biologically, fail. Death provides no fun, and pain hurts horribly. Having bodies that ward off all disease, living until we say our good-byes then translated to the next sphere, we definitely prefer to our hell where children go bald and undergo painful transfusions of bone marrow. Couldn't you just punish Adam with Eve and replace them with someone willing to be a little more patient or prevent them to try out their brilliant "shortcut," Eve's "quicker" solution?

- Giving man free will. Handing out free will likens to arming a kid with a loaded gun. And yes, he killed everyone he doesn't like.

- Honoring man's will. You have the power. Take the gun from the kid. Throw his ass into hell and tell him he can't play no more, ever.

The Father's plan changes us from slime to a son of God, from gross physical matter to a perfected spirit. Kind of crazy, don't you think? A slow train bound for a destination located on the other side of an ocean.

My thinking mirrors man's thinking, heavily influenced by Lucifer, sharing the same complaints. I'm as arrogant as Lucifer, who smirked cocksure he could come up with a better plan that takes a lot less time. I'm as impatient as Eve, who wanted to see some results after so much work. God's thinking walks a different pathway.

My Life Sucks, so God Sucks

We have cause for despair. We have justification for anger. Parents raise caring children, only to see them killed in a war. We reserve an entire section in the cemetery for children, each grave made unique by their favorite toy. Children abducted, fondled, and murdered. POWs mercilessly tortured. Divorces pile up in court like traffic violations. The drug business thrives. Gangs cruelly exterminate indiscriminately. Terrorists mass murder innocent women and children. People starve to death.

The world turned upside down, making us confused. We begin to question the value of values.

It all seems hopeless. We blame God.

God deserves no blame.

When Jesus said, "My kingdom is not of this world," I reply, "Thank God" with renewed hope. If God's kingdom looks anything like what's down here, I have zero interest; count me out.

Our situation resulted from going against God's will.

Mankind, being so backward, originated in the failures of our spiritual leaders. Unfortunately, we know little of the spiritual history of our planet. Although fragmented, much can be found in the Bible. If we knew our history better, we would no longer blame God. God cried seeing his Father's plan so screwed up and the sons he placed so much trust in turn against him or not listen.

Could God turn earth into a paradise? Yes. Could God eliminate all wars, poverty, hunger, disease, even death? Yes. Could God make everyone happy? No.

Like a spoiled child who keeps asking for more; like a troublemaking student who parents defend, like sinful behavior that society makes excuses for, these people only get worse.

Could our Heavenly Father change their behavior? God has the power to turn us into obedient slaves. And if we then have to say we love him in order to survive, what value can be found in that? Only when we freely appreciate all our Father has done for us and love him for who he is does life have any value. Our intelligence, our rationality should direct us to love our good Father. We are merely asked to wake up and see this truth.

We're in a tough-love situation and temporarily facing hardships caused by a bad older brother. If someone in your family turns out to be a child molester and serial killer, your family has to ensure that son comes to justice, and balance paternal and fraternal sympathy with the reality of choosing sin and all its consequences. The Undo button only exists on computers. The neighborhood disintegrates, no one feels safe. Fear and shock invade daily life. Our minds revert back to the days where we fend for our lives and forget about others. Where are the kids? Don't let them out of sight. Trust no one. As news spreads around the world, everyone hunkers down; we go to work then home. That's the end of the kid's sleepovers.

Who wouldn't desire their name to mean "bearer of light," yet few parents name their child Lucifer? Judas Alpheus served Jesus as a loyal apostle, yet our whole universe eschews the name because of he who betrayed Jesus.

Luckily, our Maker stood up for us and showed everyone what we could be.

If we accept that God normally works in natural ways, we will be less disappointed in the way things are today.

Watching how my parents handle their struggles provided the help I needed.

The Father used no supernatural powers to save his Son from life's hardships and allowed him to die at the hands of cruel men exhibiting behavior resembling an animal. He was able to stop all this and chose to go the "natural" way—the same for all his children.

Conclusion

If Jesus performed no miracles, Jesus's relationship as the Son of God does not change.

He raises us from the dead because, being God, he chooses to resurrect us—less a miracle and more the power of God. He put something eternal in us.

Miracle-based faith lacks survival qualities.

6

We Are Sons of God

Jesus is the Son of God.

We are sons of God, per Jesus.

So are we sons, identical to Jesus?

The quote "The distance between God and man spans such a vast gap that God could not become man" represents the thinking behind many beliefs. God can have a prophet or an advanced soul called a master to speak for him. God can spew tiny replicas named monads that incarnate, grow through varied experiences, and finally return to God like a raindrop falling back into the ocean.

1. In Christianity, God bridges the enormous gap: God becomes man, Jesus. All things are possible for God. If God can figure out how to make man, God can figure out how to become one. The reverse cannot happen; man can never become God. He can become more godlike and still retain his unique personality and identity forever.

   Christianity further believes that God's kingdom lives within us. A spiritual part of God comes down from heaven to dwell in our mind so we can know God and to help us become more like him.

2. If we don't believe in God, then man being "free" as a god would probably be the best thing going in this seemingly infinite but science-controlled universe.

   We become free in the Lucifer sense, where whatever pleases me I have the courage to go after. *Free* means total selfishness—others do not matter—and *courage* means without a conscience. Without God, conscience really becomes a false hurdle. It should be exposed as a psychological handicap introduced by parents who need control and should then be intellectually annihilated, like burning to ashes the home we grew up in. Lucifer paved this path, and many walk on it.

   The founders of the theory of communism, Karl Marx and Friedrich Engels, argued that women can be liberated from the responsibilities of motherhood and family only by finding employment outside the home. The traditional family structure oppressed women, and true family life makes true individual freedom impossible. They defined freedom and equality in line with Lucifer.

3. We can extol man, believing in the innate goodness inherent in man. If left alone without hassles, sooner or later, we realize our goodness and want to become the best that we can be. Carl Rogers and Erich Fromm stand out as the most articulate advocates I've run across.

   Both influenced me. Carl Rogers's open classroom seemed like a heavenly way of approaching teaching. It placed confidence in the good of an individual, who only needed to get a dose of freedom to make their own choices to become their best.

Something always stopped me from learning. I figured anyone can excel if they took the time. A poor student studying three hours equals a smart student studying three minutes, so grades lose meaning and are not a measurement of thinking. Subjects not offered in high school I could explore on my own I devoured. When I read Rogers's theory that I exist totally free to pursue what I want to, I rejoiced and read everything I could on psychology, especially his theories. I think a sense of freedom does unlock a door to learning. Once out of school, the subjects I loathed I pursue. Now that I don't have to memorize dates and names, history flipped to fascinating. Immersing into a classic feels like participating in an adventure once I ceased to worry about what weird essay question I'll have to wade my way through!

However, a little real-life experience, and I threw his theory away. When I applied it in a Cleveland school, I reaped pandemonium. It proved sheer folly. Rogers explained that you have to give it time, but with seconds to live, time runs out quick! The traditional lessons of self-discipline and objective testing suddenly made sense in the social setting of a classroom.

Erich Fromm expressed unbelievable faith in man. He proved man lives happier when he develops an unselfish personality. He distinguished himself as the first to identify the attributes of love. He had wonderful insights of the best in man. He wanted man to act like a son of God, but without God, reaching the apex of evolution marks the best man can achieve. Death still marks the end of life, just like any other animal. The best we can do lies in leaving a legacy that someone would want to emulate.

After reading George Orwell's *1984*—which still puts the fear of hell into me—and then seeing *1984* come alive in the Communists' relentless takeover of South Vietnam, Erich Fromm's mantle to the innate goodness of man shattered. After teaching in the Cleveland schools, I wished I trained as an army sergeant and not a philosopher king!

The teaching of man's innate goodness never goes away. We like to be positive and think the best of ourselves. The New Age movement crafts this into a keystone. We venture down here to learn and continue to evolve lifetime after lifetime until we master every lesson available to us here on earth. Knowing we can never screw up certainly has its appeal. We only stall our progress. In the worst case, we create karma for ourselves, perhaps by mass murdering a few million people. We simply did not learn our lesson. Our continuing existence guaranteed.

4. Simply deny God exists. Or, worse, attack God until eliminated from society, which we call the modern approach.

   As difficult the struggle to conceive of a God and a well-ordered universe is, a no-God conclusion makes man just another animal, one tormented with distinctive qualities.

   God exists. It's we who really don't need to.

   The existentialists explored the idea that most of us do not exist. Kierkegaard tells of the man who became so abstract in his daily life that he wakes up one morning to find he no longer exists. For the existentialist, existence means a lot more than just "being here." Mere breathing provides no evidence of life!

   We find brilliant proofs of God's existence. St. Thomas Aquinas wrote *Summa Theologica*, a volume of analytical proofs. Compared to the wisdom and understanding he gained when meditating on Jesus Christ, he viewed his work as that of a dumb ox.

   Faith comes as a gift. God dwelling within our mind arrives as a gift. Jesus appearing on earth, a gift sent from heaven. We don't reach the conclusion that God exists because of an iron-clad argument in a proof. We enjoy an unquestioned conviction. We simply know God exists by tapping into the power of God, who dwells in our own minds. Nothing can shake this faith. If I know nothing else, I know God lives.

Once we have faith, these proofs become perfectly clear and an interesting intellectual pursuit. However, Jesus taught his apostles to appeal to the spirit that lives within man. Using proofs that God exists fail in winning souls for the kingdom. We merely appeal to the intellect, which lasts until something more interesting passes through town.

Who Is Jesus?

Jesus is the Son of God. We are sons and daughters of God. The vast difference between God and a creature renders all our measuring tools obsolete.

The Son of God is God. He consists of pure spirit. He embodies total existence. He cannot not be. He always was and always will exist. He rules as sovereign. And he can create.

I don't think there is a perfect analogy for us to understand the Son of God. The situation is unique with God. God, to be a Father, must have a Son, and the love between them finds expression as the Holy Spirit—One God, three persons, no beginning and no end. Who understands this? Only God does.

If we know Jesus, we know God. To "show us the Father," Jesus answers, "You see me."

Who Are We?

Man, as an animal, can reproduce other animals.

Man transcends animals by his love for his children. God loves us. Without God, man would not love. God's loving hands holds the sons of man from their inception.

The line "The Spirit gives life" places God as the source of everything. He gives the gift of energy. An electron would not spin without energy. He gives the gift of life. My dogs would not breathe without life. He gives the gift of a soul. We would have no possibility to survive death without a soul. Spirit comes from God, like treasure secure in a safe. Fortunately, he wants to share his wealth.

God is spirit. The Spirit gives life to the world. All arrives as a gift from God, and he loves handing out gifts.

We receive spiritual gifts at conception: the gift of life—physical and spiritual—the gift of identity, the gift of mind. We open seven special gifts from the Holy Spirit and continue to rediscover these as larger presents in bigger boxes waiting for us to open them year after year, continuing throughout life.

Spiritually, at conception, we become a son or daughter of God. If his/her physical existence ceases, even when a spiritual zygote, he/she will one day be resurrected and nurtured by either surviving parents or those who need parental experience in the case of the nonsurvival of the parents. The child grows to the age where he/she can make a decision on whether to participate in God's plan or indicate "Not interested" and call it quits.

God respects the creature's will. We either desire to have a relationship with God or do not. God never coerces his creation.

At baptism, we formally celebrate a new son and daughter of God. This can be celebrated at conception, for

Christians know life begins here, but we wait to see the baby delivered and physically independent of the mother.

The baby does not yet have a soul. About the time of a child's first Communion, around age five, we make our first moral decision, and a spiritual fragment of God the Father draws near and dwells in the mind of the child. That first moral decision creates the soul, blending something material and spiritual, achieving its first permanent mark of a survival quality, a credential that survives death.

If we cooperate with our Spirit, our soul grows. We display more spiritual qualities. When Jesus advocated not traveling afar to find God for the kingdom of heaven lives within us, he referred to the fragment of the eternal Father, the God that dwells within, in our minds. When the Beatles spent a whopping percent of their wealth to travel to India for spiritual enlightenment from the Maharishi, they returned wiser men. In John Lennon's words, "We were duped."

A baby inherits the look of his parents. As he grows older, he emulates his parents in more ways. Hopefully, he reflects his parent in the habit of saying nightly prayers, going to church, telling the truth, doing volunteer work, formulating worthy goals, relaxing, and enjoying fun vacations.

In a sense, we become more of a son or daughter the more we emulate our parents. Others more easily identify us as belonging to a certain family after twelve years of living in their home than when we were born.

We exist as a son or daughter by the actions of our parents, but only through experience does sonship become more of a reality. We become a son/daughter by the actions of our heavenly parent, God, but the more we want to become like God, the more sonship becomes a living reality, a conviction we confirm through experience.

An Under Construction sign hangs over our soul, daily pouring in the decisions of man with the longings of God, mixing something material with something spiritual. Angels faithfully record any cooperation achieved between man and God. A new substance forms beyond the physical realm that makes us look more like a son of God. When a soul finally fuses with the spiritual fragment of God the Father, we will look even more like a son of God. As we become more spirit, at each step in our sojourn of the universe, we look even more like God's son. Others readily recognize our Dad in us.

If we study the stages of a baby's formation: the moment of conception—the tiny brain, little body, Lilliputian organs, appearance of fingernails—on to our birth, we discover an analogy to the formation of a son of God. However, a newborn has more in common with his earthly parents than with God or God's Son. Not until our resurrection do we spiritually achieve a place in the universe comparable to a baby's birth as we begin in a new, less-material world. Our spiritual growth in this life resembles more the development of a fetus.

Of course, our own son may desire to have nothing to do with us. He owns that free-willed choice. Likewise, we may want nothing to do with God. He allows us a 100 percent free-willed choice to no longer be his son or daughter. The spirit of God within retains all the good in the lifetime and departs, and there remains nothing of worth left.

We start at the bottom of the chart. It took millions of years of evolution to create man, a creature capable of will. It will take us millions of years seeking God to become perfect. Jesus said to be perfect even as our Heavenly Father is perfect. We belong to the order of the Ascending Sons of God: start at the bottom, work our way to the top. We learn a great deal and grow into perfect beings, light-years from where we find ourselves now both in physical distance and spiritual growth. God will always be infinitely greater than us. We will be able to make a more accurate assessment of this difference in greatness, perfection, goodness, beauty, truth, and every other aspect of God that we will better understand.

God also creates beings as nearly perfect representations of him. God directly creates divine but less-than-perfect beings. These sons and daughters come down to help lesser sons and daughters. They belong to the order of the Descending Sons of God.

One Father fills a whole universe with kids. Each child is different and possesses various levels of divinity and perfection.

The eldest son follows in his father's footsteps and becomes a physician, the middle daughter works in home improvement, and the youngest learns slowly and is not likely to go out on his own without a lot of help; the father loves them all.

Even God's direct creations can go their way because of free will.

Life comes with no guarantees. Sonship can end, and a gift can be returned. God respects our will. If we wish to end a relationship, we can. If we desire to know God more, we will succeed.

I was my parents' son; never questioned it.

In the same way, we are God's son.

It becomes more obvious once we become spirit.

Conclusion

Hey, kid, your dad is God, and will be for all eternity.

He doesn't think you're worthless. He loves you.

You've got a career, a home, and a family with him. Get that set in your mind, and get through this life. Try to be more like him.

You found the gold nugget. We call this the faith.

7

Man Is Evil

"Sin wins"—a summary of nearly every newspaper article repeated daily.

Man has one strike against him: himself when he chooses sin.

Take a nation of great intelligence and Christian compassion. One day, a man enjoys dinner with his neighbor. The next day, he turns them in to be exterminated. His day job includes the gassing and disposing of children. In the evening, he plays baseball with his kids. Darkness overtook Germany.

A professor of English enjoys *The Great Gatsby*. The next day, she's arrested for teaching literature of the great Satan. The grand culture of Persia dissolved into the dark Islam Republic of Iran.

Two neighbors reminisce over their long friendship since they were small boys, sipping banana beer. The next day, one slaughters the other with a machete, calling him a cockroach. Rwanda.

I tell my class the lights shine too bright and turn half off. They adjust to less light. I say there's still too much light and put them in total darkness. After a short time, they get used to the darkness.

I light a match and say, "Jesus said, 'I am the light of the world.'" At first, we find the flame offensive and the brightness leaves our eyes impaired, but we see clearly we were in darkness. They never asked to have the lights turned off but were told it would be better for them to have the lights off.

We now understand how sin works. It works the same everywhere.

I've become way too fat. I look in the mirror and don't see myself as huge. When the other pregnant guy left the workout room, I stepped on the scale. A scientific scale probably measures accurately, so I can't use that argument. I don't think I can change anything in my life, so I'll live with being corpulent and continue to enjoy life consuming hot and greasy hamburgers.

That's how I handle subtle sin too.

Sin makes dying more serious, but making a big change, like not watching TV, may be sacrificing too much.

I witness managers demean others, choosing perception over truth until the victim loses his livelihood. If born in Rwanda, would they be carrying a machete?

I hardly sleep after two nights in subzero weather on a Boy Scout Klondike. I have a shorter fuse and not many happy thoughts. How many days more before I lose it?

Many are civil if they have what they want. When we lose amenities, most turn ugly rather quickly.

Goodness can be a tenuous facade. If I lost my possessions, I could stoically figure I still have my life and health and so would be unaffected. When I actually lost a restaurant and was held responsible for a $300,000 loan and expecting to lose my house and cars and everything I worked for, I shattered, devastated. Hard experience taught me I measured up hardly as noble as I imagined myself to be.

If we were born in Germany, how many would ease into key positions in the "New hope: I promise change" Nazi Party? We can visualize numerous persons, if placed in that time and place, fulfilling a Nazi seamlessly. We dislike a breadwinner and callously eliminate his job along with his pride. We ignore the fact that he provides the sole financial support to his family and has advanced in age. With limited chances of finding a job, he's done—all handled effortlessly, like meeting a quota to make the company or society stronger.

Humans born today do not inherit qualities superior to those born before reaching adulthood in Nazi Germany. They are just not living in Nazi Germany. The enigma of why the Holocaust happened should be amended as why it doesn't happen more often.

We wish we were alive to meet Jesus as a human on earth. We imagine ourselves as close followers. Most people of that time wanted to put Jesus to death. I'd bet we'd probably join the mob rather than put ourselves in harm's way.

I suspect if we sent the managers of government and those with a disturbed conscience to Vietnam in place of those who did go atrocities would have skyrocketed.

Will future historians portray Jane Fonda as unbelievably naive or immoral? Jane Fonda bears responsibility for the torture and death of American POWs while visiting Communist leaders whom she sympathized with.

Mel Brooks quipped in *Space Balls* that being good is a stupid approach! The cleaner we break open a kernel of truth, the more we laugh. When in the heart of a joke we see situations we experienced and then see someone else handle it much worse, it strikes us funnier. Although I laughed at Mel's line in the Star Wars parody, I don't in real life. Evil keeps one-upping us. Evil runs circles around most of us.

I served as a juror on a criminal case. I listened to the prosecutor and agreed with everything he said. I listened to the defense and agreed with everything he said. They both sounded true and contradicted each other.

Evil often seems distant, like some mythological dragon living in a far-off land. Distance makes men brave, too far away to hear or care about the plight of others. We prefer to pretend evil does not exist. I've seen it. I've experienced it. I know evil exists. I wish it did not exist and did not affect me. I try to ignore it.

I handle death the same way. I don't think about it. I forget it will occur. I pretend it will not happen to me.

Good people take up their cross daily and try to do their best. Their concerns center on their family. They work hard to provide a good home. They try to become better persons. They avoid complaining and make the best of their situation. Striving for something better that will make their children's and sometimes other children's lives a little easier.

Unexpectedly, we slip into a black hole. At times, as if by fate, the black hole appears under our feet.

That's how it seems to me. We were innocent children, reminiscing of birthday parties with smiling parents, gifts to celebrate our birth, the excitement and magic of Christmas, warmth in the arms of a mother, our family close together praying to the baby Jesus, following a rule book of clear morals, and receiving ready forgiveness.

Then a new reality that did not seem real intruded. A living nightmare that emerged too harsh, too cruel, and too inhuman. A world filled with fear and terror. Orwell's *1984* admonitions arrived, early but accurate. Could any of us conceive the idea of a twelve-year-old boy taken from his parents to practice head shots, conscripted in the North's army until killed or victory won?

We tried to ignore the horror of Vietnam. We were afraid of friends who came back like they were survivors of the Holocaust. We were afraid my brother or I would be sent and never return alive. I was smaller, so I'd have to go in the tunnels where a poisonous snake waited, tied up, positioned to strike me in my face. Our family trembled and ate meals in silence.

Terror and evil grabbed hold of the world. People we did not understand raised fists at us, some in our own backyard.

As I walk through the halls of the inner city school where I taught, I contemplate that some evil plotter did all he could to destroy the children and then realized he couldn't surpass what they do to themselves.

One could get high walking the halls when a new marijuana shipment arrives. Every teacher experiences wasted class time dealing with students, talking out loud whenever they had something to say to a friend, paying no attention, not caring, impulsively fighting, or showing off dad's shotgun to the class. Community leaders visit our brand-new school where wanton destruction ran rampant: willful breaking of toilets, defacing walls, smashing glass. To look into our eyes and lie seems habitual. It left adults wondering if students were even aware of doing what they were just caught doing.

There were students so dissolute we couldn't help but hope that the cruel streets will take care of them, meaning to end their lives.

If I blamed this on the devil, I would think of myself as a fundamentalist who uses the Bible instead of his brain. Every college-educated person knows we can explain bad behavior by the unfavorable conditions they endured.

But the majority of students acted with good intentions, revealing strong moral values, and excelled. Some rose exemplary out of the dirty environment like a phoenix with beautiful feathers rising out of the ashes, possessing a strong character.

Conditions influence them, but their choices determine their direction.

Imagine someone who only thinks about gaining power every second of his or her life. Imagine someone who plots against others, making this their main focus. Imagine a brilliant, super-advanced someone doing this for two hundred thousand years. This one powerful personality first introduced corrupt thinking that continues to confuse our thinking. His ceaseless efforts constantly burden our lives. Evil doesn't think the same way as good. And worse, evil takes any path to reach its end.

I detect an insidious plot that I cannot put my finger on. I can point to its many successes.

As a teacher, I wondered what I would do different in schools if I actually desired to harm my inner-city students rather than try to do them good. I'd tweak or accelerate a few programs but not change much.

I wondered if the evil in the world maps into milestones of a master plan or is the result of mankind simply experimenting and learning to leave behind a backward past.

What if I intentionally wanted to keep the students dumb?

I'd ignore differences. I'd designate discrimination (differential treatment) as evil. I'd eliminate student ratings. I'd insist that every student belongs in a classroom.

One student can disrupt an entire class, and five to fifty minutes of learning evaporates. If we don't handle the 1 percent of thugs and antisocial people, the school will survive only for free lunches instead of a place of learning.

We hear the same student names over and over in the teachers' lounge. They must spend their day going from class to class, causing disruptions.

The school system classified the student body in groups labeled 1 to 10. The 1's were the brightest, most intelligent, and well behaved. They were overall the top students. They stood as models, so students strived to become a 1, seeing this as their own best pathway.

Who would place a 1 and 10 in the same class citing equal treatment?

After ruminating on how to harm students, the schools implemented my no-longer-fanciful list.

In the seventies, we denounced all discrimination as bad. This continues today with an updated set of mantras: there is nothing you can't do or be, all will benefit through inclusion, diversity guarantees success. We built a modern tower of Babel.

Schools eliminate ratings. We shuffle the cards and accept that an ace has the same value as any other card. In my algebra class, bright students become bored, and the challenged student—some not knowing their multiplication tables—sit hopelessly lost. They share confusion equally.

Totalitarian leaders give us better insight into evil.

Lucifer provides the most influential legacy of evil left here on earth. He fostered insurrection in order to rule in place of God.

His first tenet took root: "God does not exist." Like a myth, religious leaders conjure up a god to keep man obedient and prevent him from doing whatever gives man pleasure.

Lucifer's platform boasted to set man free. His followers advertised his ubiquitous slogan "A friend of man." No one should be told that he or she couldn't do something or be something that they wanted to be. Why follow rules that restrain? Have the guts to rebel against the existing powers that curb our desires and personal preferences.

Weapons

Evil stockpiles the world's largest arsenal of weapons.

Confusion proves lethal. That gentle eroding of values and moral positions and heroes and right versus wrong makes every spiritual war a Vietnam. Will the wearing down of values prove disastrous? Look at the Grand Canyon. Should those stalwart hunks of rock left standing above the raging river be admired or deigned too stupid to foresee their eventual fate?

Good and evil remains simple for people living checklist lives. The well-off Pharisees delineated every life event against their established list of rules. These people wanted nothing to do with Jesus and his indefinable love.

Since our thoughts have been heavily influenced by the thinking of Lucifer as he convinced so many on earth that "we need dramatic changes to make life better for all," confusion settles as a natural state for most of us.

If I chose evil, I'd want Jesus eliminated. I want any remnant of God expunged. I'd want love to die.

Evil wants to do the following: (a) kill people, (b) screw people, (c) kill God, and (d) kill God completely; that is, to eliminate the attributes of God—truth, beauty, and goodness. Exterminate any visage of love.

Begin with the killers. Use them to eliminate people of faith. Nero rules as my masterpiece; his only concern happened to be his harp being out of tune. Any progress to report, gentlemen? What's the battle plan? I need ideas, people!

We target civilians: women, children, the rich, the poor. Mass murder in the name of God.

A perfect blaspheme, attributing to God something unreal to him. Superb twist! Make God a murderer, murder for the sake of murder. Why did I limit who gets killed? Continue to use every trick to secure a killer's freedom so he can serve us. Create hopelessness in those enforcing the law. Prove that evil wins.

We hold the trumps, play them! Always attack. Keep the enemy on the defensive. With arrogance, represent questionable facts as unquestionable, feign righteous indignation, interrupt continually, and insist on your right of free speech to keep our ideas on the front page. Force our lies into other's minds through peer pressure, media, and repetition.

Downplay and mock heroes. Tear down what they accomplish, substitute honorable motives with suggested personal gains, and criticize any use of force. Blur moral distinctions, and show contempt to those who suggest subtle differences. Broadcast invidious feelings as progress in tolerance by getting it out in the open, which helps discourage real achievements.

Convince citizens to lay down their guns, and we won't have to fight. Our KGB's brainstorm, a "war for peace," wins over millions of minions each year. Drugs render them helpless weaklings. Multiple languages assure distrust. Muddle minds any way we can.

Destroy marriage by redefining a family as individuals with personal goals. Promote women at work under the ideal of diversity and making up for a lack of opportunity in the past. Let them be the bosses of men. Let them be self-sufficient and not need men. Destroy the marriage institution by displacing man as the breadwinner. When woman becomes man's serious competitor, he will lose any affection for her; she turns into another male. Ingrained in our evolution to survive, she becomes a fierce rival, taking away his family's source of food.

Destroy the maternal instinct. Abort early before mother suckles the baby. Our success rate to kill a child after being suckled remains low, even in primitives maternal affection kicks in. Cut the human—oops, use the word *glob*—in the womb to keep it impersonal, as pressing a button to drop a bomb seems easier than stabbing someone while looking into one's eyes. They must never figure out there exists no difference spiritually between destroying a fetus, a newborn, or a child who is four years old as neither yet has made a moral decision.

"Personal liberty" lives on as our leaders' battle cry. Emphasize that the woman owns her body and can do what best suits her needs.

Take Orwell to heart. He figured out our future plans. Convince people that fiction serves only to entertain. Meanwhile, his warnings can serve as our goals.

Lack of knowledge assures our stability. Keep people concerned only about their petty daily problems and jobs, and we grow stronger. Progress?

Using the equality banner, we burden students. We mix advanced students in with those lacking basic skills. Inclusion prevents both from learning.

We made equality a sacred act, causing eyes to glaze and brains to short-circuit.

The majority always forget someone will rule. Equality sounds so good, who would not desire to have every human equal? We comply, making them equally helpless, listless, an impoverished indistinguishable mass of humanity to assure our kingdom rules earth.

We renamed cutthroat ambition "soft skills" to render education and hard work nonessential. Professionals know less about their subject and more about managing our propaganda. Teachers no longer achieve expertise with a master's in mathematics, English, or chemistry, only a master's in education, where we convince them of the importance of inclusion. Put top engineers under the tutelage of professional managers proud they are clueless in engineering. Bury Deming's teamwork where the manager helps and knows the most. Instead, create a Pharisaic structure that burdens productive workers with methodologies, endless paperwork and approvals, government scrutiny, deadlines guaranteeing oppressive overtime; compromise quality; and show no concern for a worker's welfare. On the contrary, treat nonkey laborers as workhorses whom we send to the glue factory when done.

Dishearten leaders who do make decisions. Disdain the productive as fools for not offloading their work to others. Thankfully, *Atlas Shrugged* contains so many pages no one reads it!

Morals enslave us. Accepting law and responsibility that go with freedom really ties our hands. We need unlicensed freedom. Any steps forward?

We blur true freedom, painting responsibility to others as a drag. We teach that no one should be subject to laws, only those who don't think out of the box—our latest excuse for feeling superior. We put the mentally ill back on the streets. We teach disdain for law enforcement and assail them for not respecting people who flail menacingly and spit on them. Personal liberty still succeeds as our founding fathers' greatest wile to destroy a democracy.

Good! Let me stress we must overthrow governments and put ourselves in power. Interpret their Bill of Rights against them. I want to establish these as the law of the land: the baby inside a mother is simply property she owns. Drugs legalized; pose as an anticrime measure. A moral-neutral acceptance for doing whatever pleases oneself, arguing the expression of one's individuality overrides everything. Arrest anyone who disagrees with us, accusing them of hate crime. Deal a dirty hand, and they won't know what to do!

And our usual winner? Never forget, when they make war, we can relax.

War focuses the object of hate away from us. Let them fight one another. Teach leaders to wage war even when no real enemy exists to secure their power. Channel hatred. Build up through fabricated reports, and like a pressure cooker, release frustration at a rally to help instill mass hysteria.

Remember our advanced skills, tapping into primal fear and self-survival. Suggest that everyone needs more. Whoever controls the media controls men's minds. We may even get elected! Then we model *1984* with a dash of *Brave New World*, whatever allows us to take over and make the rest to be of no importance except to serve the one government that "protects them," which, in reality, protects our power.

For man, evil keeps winning. For God, good always wins. However, unless we join God's side, evil will rule our planet. Man can make earth a living hell and then die off and be forgotten. Not God's plan but man's current pursuit.

My parents never viewed me as evil. Since evil pervades our world, they were worried. That's why I received the sacraments. That's why we went to confession every Saturday. That's why we went to church. They knew I would be on my own and hoped my spiritual foundation would withstand the immoral bombardments.

God knows the mere presence of evil differs from sin. The free will of man chooses sin; evil exists only because of goodness, like a shadow exists only because of the light. Our struggles being difficult and the phenomena of so much sinfulness down here derive from key players scrapping God's plan.

We continue—although stupid, suicidal, and we are heading toward the annihilation of our own personality—to choose sin. Why we do may be linked to Freud's discovery of a death wish, which ironically also marks us separate from an animal.

And so our heavenly parents go in search of lost ones. They drop everything in order to bring us back. They rejoice when we return. What shepherd does not leave the ninety-nine sheep and search for the one lost? What parent does not throw a party when his son returns?

Jesus said, "I have not come to condemn men but to save them."

Jesus understands that men who embrace sin exist only in this short life and then are gone forever.

Conclusion

The devil does exist but cowers impotent before the power of God. If we have faith, the devil will not draw near.

Those who reject God and embrace evil do the works of Lucifer. They harvest the fruit of the seeds planted by Lucifer on earth many years ago. Powerful devils roaming the earth seize the opportunity and successfully use these people.

The relationship seems more like joining a gang than a possession. Without God, we watch man crawl back to the slime pool and reenact scenes from our evolutionary past.

The problem deduces to humans going it alone without God, slowly getting used to sinning until finally embracing iniquity.

We live with evil. As soon as good existed, the potential to not be good existed. Evil can only tempt us.

Lucifer's thinking embedded into our family's thinking, being our older brother who turned bad. I still hear and see his signature works everywhere. When I can't spot them, I set aside some time for an examination of conscience.

I get used to looking through eyeglasses with smudges, scratches, and paint splatters. I succumb to "At least I can see" vision. I tell my wife, "You're kidding! You can read that billboard?" I'm lucky to make out the billboard.

Evil always justifies itself. Stalin believed he did nothing wrong, just running a country. Certainly, we would never do what Stalin did. But then again, we're not running a country.

What we call a successful life—being professional, being courteous, going to work every day, donating money to charity, and being involved in our children's activities—does not contribute to our survival. We merely become a modern Nicodemus. Only if we know Christ, and do these things for Christ, can we labor assured of our present and eternal future.

The philosopher Kierkegaard and the poet T. S. Eliot warned us about evasions. Anything but Christ falls under an evasion. Only in Christ can we find life, for he is the way, the truth, and the life.

A lesser devil, Caligastia, is over two hundred billion years old. He has a couple of hundred advanced degrees from the universe's top schools in the study of man and on how he thinks. There exists a good chance that he can outsmart any of us. Naturally he looks for the brightest or most powerful and lets them win the rest over. If one is at the top of some human achievement and doesn't believe in God and an afterlife and the devil's existence, how easy it is to hand over one's soul for a carrot of enhanced hubris with increased power over more people.

How many good people unwittingly do Caligastia's work?

I foresee the Holocaust museums adding an Abortion Wing in the future. The focus shifts from horrible leaders to families who allowed on this "world of the cross" the murder of their own babies.

8

Man Is Good

You're kidding, right? Reread the prior chapter and quit.

It doesn't take much to convince me that this world deserves a Hopeless rating, and correctly so, as long as man remains the only factor.

God equals hope. No other source exists.

We really evolved from a slime pool. We developed into superior animals due to our brain. We can formulate three approaches to our existence:

1. Celebrate being an animal. Enjoy the flesh. Rise to the top. Become the leader of the pack.

    A conscience gets in the way. Only power matters.

2. Celebrate being human. Be the best one can be. Improve your mind, body, and emotional stability, and maintain a positive outlook.

3. Celebrate being a son or daughter of God. Realize God's hand in all this. Through evolution and experience, we advance, our hand in God's hand, being led on an eternal adventure.

Like a sieve, we see how well these categories shake out:

1. Celebrate being an animal.

    Gain physical power. Be beautiful by working out, putting on cosmetics, wearing designer clothes, and paying with plastic for plastic surgery. Use your body to attract sexual partners. Pose for a decent check. Think Hollywood.

    Gain material power. Enjoy a huge house, vacations, gourmet food, and quality wine. Concentrate on a career to make money and be financially influential; own more than others. Gain political power. Possess power for the sake of power. Torture and kill anyone whom you don't trust. Only feed the army, and they'll do your bidding. If in a democratic country, appeal to those who have the most votes.

    The most successful win hallmarks in history books, sharing pages with the Hitler's, Saddam Hussein's, and Joseph Stalin's. They saw clearly the desired end and eliminated anything standing in the way. They reign as king reducing others to servants. Totalitarians keep it simple: whatever it takes to remain in power. If God did not exist, this makes the most sense.

2. Celebrate being human.

    Man's happiness blossoms by helping others. Become your best, and by personal achievements, mankind too will benefit.

Positive Thinking

Control your thoughts to always be happy. Avoid negative thinking and thinkers. We alone assume responsibility for our happiness or sadness. Calm our minds through meditation and yoga. Contemplate the peace of a star in the universe, and breathe in harmony with nature and our fellow creatures.

Visualize ourselves wealthy and content, and we will bring money and satisfaction into our lives. By the power of our mind, we will attract whatever we visualize. This works by the mystical law of attraction, for "thoughts are things." Or we can study the lives of successful people and distill the qualities they possess and emulate them, and we should soon follow in their footsteps. Here we use logic to discover the secret to another's success.

These popular topics sell since they promise to open the door to personal success.

A Positive Man

All things work out for our benefit because God plans everything for our own good.

We come down to earth to learn and grow. We are all a part of God—tiny monads or souls that desire to incarnate to speed up our growth.

We don't sin. We make mistakes and pursue wrong paths. We face good and bad experiences from our preplanned lessons packed with karma factored in and perfectly placed in our lives. We confront a situation and learn, by going through it, to undertake the best path. Enlightenment comes from lifetimes of experiences and learning from each consequence. No one begins better than anyone else; they're simply an older soul. We continue to reincarnate until we get it right.

The differences in people, the disparity in our lives, depend on what lessons we need to learn. Maybe it's how to handle wealth, or we may need to learn how to survive in poverty. Each encounter helps us grow. Karma results from how we handle relationships with our fellow travelers. If we are harsh to our children, we become the child of a draconian parent—our children from our past life. That wonderful aunt who keeps looking out for us, we were kind to in a prior life.

We will be successful. We return into the tapestry like a piece of colored thread in the complex and beautiful design we call God.

This novel thinking that we name the New Age actually flows from an ancient wisdom long known in India. The camera focuses in on a person's life, albeit ever encouraging that man to serve others and become more perfect.

In psychology, Carl Rogers postulates that once man realizes his own freedom to explore any subject on earth, he finds the key to learning, and that sense of freedom ignites into flames of curiosity. Erich Fromm concludes we attain happiness only when participating in the best man can offer: love. He analyzed love as an art form that applies the human traits of care, respect, responsibility, and knowledge. Since these are learnable, achievement lies in our hands.

In twentieth-century philosophy, the existentialists tried to come to man's aid.

After two world wars, the definition of man as a "rational animal" no longer worked. Shocked by man's atrocities and feeling abandoned, the time seemed right to throw everything away and start from scratch. If man had any values left, we must begin by realizing that they are not rooted in anything. After witnessing a Nazi doctor performing surgery on children fully awake to graph pain thresholds, mankind knew there was nothing left. Despair leaves God out cold. The innate goodness of man proved not credible. How does man all alone, his very existence an absurd and questionable state, find dignity? He must admit his nonbeing and take action to find his own meanings, though subjective and irrelevant.

We can strive to exist as our best and only achievement. We attained an honest assessment of life without God.

In sociology, the overemphasis of service overwhelms. We seek to fill the void of emptiness within, like pouring water into a sieve—what the existentialists call nothingness.

We expect high school students to volunteer excessive hours because colleges peruse for community-minded candidates. So essentially, they are forced to work for free for the good of the country in order to get into college. The line between forced labor and social service fades indistinct. Without God, they become the same.

In the final analysis, we perfect ourselves and serve others to feel better about ourselves. Without God, even helping our brothers degrades into a selfish act, our motive being to think better of ourselves.

3. Celebrate being a son or daughter of God.

Do we even grasp this, let alone celebrate? As a child, I loved having a birthday and couldn't wait for my party. I sure look forward to a family vacation, of getting away from the grind and seeing something new.

The intimate relationship of sonship to God demands time to digest the reality and work through the implications. It helps to be a parent. That explains why God plans for everyone to raise children either here on earth or immediately after.

Growing up in the fifties proved to be a blessed time. My mother's job demanded assurance that I remain happy and continue growing up as a good boy. That entailed her full-time job.

We kids had it pretty good. I have only fond memories.

We ate like kings. I've yet to find a restaurant that served so tasty a main course and so many choices. Everything packed a rich and full flavor. My mom utilized all fat, grease, and remnant pieces-parts in one meal or another. She added and re-added garlic, onions, and natural juices to every dish. At Easter, the skin and top two inches of fat from a pig hung in our garage. We'd cut off pieces with the paprika, coating and eat it raw. Later, we'd sit around a fire and catch the hot drippings of grease on bread and—with onions, cucumbers, and additional applications of hot fat—eat, drink, and talk.

Every Saturday morning I'd walk to St. Thomas More for catechism. Along the way, we stopped at Mike's grocery store. After a friendly greeting, we'd buy baseball cards with the flat, hard stick of gum in the packet. We find pop bottles in the creek and get a nickel a bottle from him. At Halloween, he'd let us pick up our favorite candy bar. What a guy!

As we crossed the street, the Honey Ice Cream store beckoned. The owner kept bees and mixed the honey in with his homemade ice cream. Don't think anyone else had thought of adding honey at this time. He put in a lot of honey, and the ice cream tasted sweet and absolutely delicious.

The house on the corner where we turned down to the church grew a huge buckeye tree positioned near the sidewalk, and the only Ohio state tree I'd ever seen. I'd love to take a souvenir of the different stages of the fruit—with a green covering, partially out, and the dark-brown buckeye itself.

In school, I took my classes seriously, bringing home a suitcase of books then back. I did some homework, but it never occurred to me to study. I just listened in class and could not believe someone expected me to spend hours doing homework, so I only turned in homework for classes that penalized me for not doing it. One friend got all As on algebra tests, refused to do homework, and received an F. He refused to change his stance and failed algebra; he deserved an A.

In high school, the smarter kids delved into philosophy. The top brain read Sartre and pursued starting a philosophy club to discuss how to be free and other ideas. A classmate who walked home the same route read Nietzsche. I think being of German descent he decided Nietzsche stood out as the best. I read tidbits and commented that he stood against Christ, how can he think such things? He told me I read so little philosophy I did not understand. I ignored the put-down, but now I can see his point.

Through the influence of PSR and Christian movies, I came to look upon the priesthood as the most important job in the world. Everyone works for manna, for things that perish. This man saves souls.

Every action in those days had moral implications. Every thought had moral implications. We grew up going to church every Sunday and to confession every Saturday night. I evaluated my actions and thoughts.

The war in childhood we waged to always be good. Teachers educated us about sin based on the Ten Commandments. We held a powerful and clear solution to an error: confession.

To people on the front lines, identifying sin borders on the impossible. As we struggle to make a living, nothing seems simple morally.

As we grow up, relationships become more important, especially close ones.

My son and daughter don't confess sins to me or prepare a speech before conversing. We both want to keep a loving, happy relationship and naturally do whatever that takes. We speak freely and truthfully with one another.

God choose to be our eternal Father, our Father in this life and in the next. That makes us his sons and daughters.

We know this relationship from our earth family, and the more loving our father, the closer the bond. With God, this same relationship takes on deeper and more perfect qualities. It necessarily becomes our most important relationship, lasting for eternity.

If we had good and loving parents, the idea of God being a loving parent becomes easier for us to understand. If we experience being parents, we may realize some of our decisions toward our children resemble God's decisions toward his children—us.

The family forms the foundation of society, civilization, and our spiritual understanding of God.

We—being spiritual sons and daughters of a loving Father, the good news of Jesus—wholly depend upon the experience of loving relationships in our own family for us to fully appreciate its meaning in our lives here on earth.

Good family experiences give children an edge: the advantage of knowing God, who is all good.

My parents thought of me as a good kid. They always saw the best in me and my future potential. Our Heavenly Parent sees even more possibilities far more clearly.

Our Heavenly Father planned a future for us full of happiness and self-satisfaction.

Since God dwells in our minds, we find something good and perfect within us that awaits, ever hoping we join forces.

Conclusion

Can we call man good? Man, in liaison with God, becomes good. Alone, he's nothing worthwhile.

Master architects designed man's evolution. They knew every genetic combination and planned every mutation. They gave us impressive-working physical bodies.

Man's mind comes as a gift from God. The Holy Spirit gives a fetus a mind at conception. Consider it on loan.

Man's personality comes as a gift of God, each permutation as unique as our retina.

Man's spirit comes as a gift of God. God the Father sends a fragment of himself to dwell in our minds.

Man's ability to know the truth comes as a gift of God. Jesus poured his own Spirit of Truth over all of mankind at Pentecost. That same spirit waits for us today if we but desire his presence.

Man's hope for goodness, for eternal survival, lies totally in the power of God.

When you factor in meaningless murders, jealousy, and greed, it can be argued that man, without God, marks below the animal world.

And even with God, my golden retriever exhibits qualities hard to beat!

9

Woman's Greatest Achievement Is Raising Children

Parents show great love as they sacrifice for their children.

A mother who spends 24-7 caring for her children sacrifices her life for others. We find no greater love, says Jesus.

No one can do the job of a mother who stays home and raises her children. Others can do the job of a woman working outside the home.

Reasons Why Woman Should Stay Home

1. In the first years, a child's foundation sets. He/she establishes his entire perception of the universe. Mothers can make or break the success of a child's eternal career.

   A baby's brain works like a sponge: he/she absorbs everything they come in contact with. Although an old expression, new discoveries reveal the impressiveness of this tiny organ as it can soak up an ocean of information if given the opportunity.

Berlitz, of the learning-languages fame, heard multiple languages in his home since he was a baby. Knowing languages became second nature. I've heard Polish spoken for thirty years as an adult and recognize no words except *piwo*, meaning "beer." My wife listened as a baby. When she attended college in Krakow, everyone assumed she lived there.

I see infomercials of two-year-olds identify pictures, saying the correct word due to early exposure of picture/word associations.

Babies who listen to classical music possess advanced learning skills. Even plants grow better.

These proofs come from scientific studies. They measure the improved motor and cognitive skills of a baby. They only scratch the surface on the effect on a baby.

The first couple of years on earth influences a child's entire life and afterlife. "Is the universe friendly?" We answer as a baby. They will be accepting and trusting of the overcare of God throughout their eternal career or be untrusting for a long, long time. Their first year of life could retard their spiritual progress for literally a million years.

Infants go through a stage where they stop playing and go to their mothers for a hug. They need to be reassured and then return to their play contented. They do this multiple times a day.

Their attitude of what the world holds for them—a mother giving us a hug and then holding out her hand to safely lead us, or "We're in this alone, and no one really cares"—forms and deeply sets like concrete by the fifth year. At the center of the personality lies a permanent warm spot or a permanent cold spot.

Many working women cite the success of their children's careers as proof of the value of enabling their children to become independent at a very young age. If you leave your children every day for a career, one lesson cries out clearly to children: nothing on earth ranks over a career, not even them. Naturally they dedicate their lives to a career. They measure their value as a person by success in their career.

Forcing children to take responsibility, along with the draconian consequences of the child's nonadult behavior, begins taking precedence over compassionate understanding and maternal love. Mothers tire after so much time spent away from home. Discipline provides an ethical lesson easily and quickly. Patience and forgiveness travel into the spiritual realm and take years to learn. God intended the mother to hand spiritual values down from generation to generation. Woman dropping this torch results in dire consequences.

2. You are the only right person for the job.

You love the child more than anyone else on earth. No one can do as good a job as you to raise this child. No one possesses the love that you have. No one cares more than you. No one invested more than you. You've cared for another human for nine months and then suffered so the baby can be born.

Women bear the biologic disadvantage of carrying a baby for a long nine months and then undergoing birth. The design will not suffer change. God intended it.

The pregnancy provides a time of waiting, anticipation, joy, and contemplation.

Normal instincts involve us to care for and protect—with one's own life, if necessary—this new life totally depending on me. The Heavenly Father allows us to share in the act of creation that resides in his power alone. He wants us to know the joy of having sons and daughters. He wants us to better understand him and to want to become more like him, a perfect parent.

God acts as a loving parent whom we can rely on. His universe that we will traverse requires our love and trust; that alone allows us to proceed further and to succeed in our future. This capacity a mother imparts to her children by offering her life, her everything to them. In the first five years, mothers open the door to a complete understanding of God's love. Such children pass God's "exams" with flying colors!

The Holy Spirit serves as a good mother throughout our life. The Holy Spirit, whom we know so little about, acts as a she, a maternal being here on earth. This being never makes her presence known. Rather, she makes known the presence of the Son, Jesus. And the Son speaks only of his Father.

Some mothers stay always there for us. They forget about themselves and are only concerned about their kids. We don't spend much time thinking about our mothers. We take them for granted until they pass. Then their love becomes clear, and we have lost an eternity. The only event that compares, probably, would be if we lose eternity; the Ancients of Days adjudge us as a nonsurvival candidate.

The hand that rocks the cradle controls destiny. A mother's hand forms the physical, moral, and spiritual destiny of her child.

Only a mother can raise her child. God provided no substitute to the presence of a mother. Her absence creates an imbalance. Handing the job over to church or secular always fails. As the child's tears harden, the encrustation manifests as a fanatic clinging to religious rules, leading to hypocrisy or a strictly business material-gain approach to relationships.

Nurturing cannot be done after a day's work. The opportunity to raise your babies happens once; if missed, accept it as gone forever.

3. No guilt.

If you stayed home to raise your children, you did everything possible to give your son or daughter a good foundation. If they stray, by their own free will, they chose badly. Pray that they receive the gift of wisdom.

The parental experience, raising a child to maturity, tops the list of requirements that must be met before we proceed in our own universe career. Everyone must raise children; how else can we grasp what the sentence "God as our parent" truly means?

I don't know if this will happen, but I would not want to be the mother or father of children and told after being resurrected that I lack the experience of raising children. Having had the opportunity and failing certainly differs from never having had the opportunity.

4. Equal, not the same.

The sexes differ in every way. We were meant to complement each other as "the other," like a circle with a diameter line drawn. As a couple, we improve our chances to succeed. No combination turns out more productive than a man and a woman.

Usurping man's role continues even though foolhardy and leads to disaster.

In the late 1970s, I travelled Europe. I met two young women from Belgium on the train. They surprised me by asking, "What's wrong with American women? They've become masculine. They even have deep voices." I, of course, never noticed until I spent time with these two women.

They were kinder and easier to talk to and friendly to be with. They were headed into careers, but that seemed secondary to them.

My mind-set formulated that Europe lags behind and that in ten or twenty years their industry will catch up and they will be just like us. It never dawned on me that they made a conscious decision to not become like us! They love to sit with neighbors in a sidewalk café after work. They desire to know others as part of their education and, thus, provide time to travel.

A gentleman in Luxembourg asked if he could be of service—in five languages. I stammered, dumbfounded, and finally managed to say, "English!" A courteous, service-oriented attitude, plus knowing five languages, laid as a foundation before one even starts their studies in a chosen career! This humbled me.

Europeans play everything but catch-up. They possess a will to preserve their choice of people and values first, with a lifestyle that promotes making living worthwhile.

I'm not blind to some lack of success in maintaining these values and to the reluctance to participate in the wider world of men today.

For thousands of years, man provided the needs to survive, and woman made that survival worthwhile through home and children. These roles civilized man. The marriage bond ascended as the crowning achievement of human evolution. The founding of the home solidified into the keystone of society.

When competitors attempted to usurp a man's food source, he killed them. His hatred toward them could be deemed essential to his own and to his family's survival.

God never intended woman to be man's serious competitor. She proved herself fully capable but became another man in the process. As she takes over the livelihood of man, she has become man's enemy and the enemy of that man's family. The relationship of man and woman necessarily turns cold and devoid of chivalry. Men soon forget affectionate emotions reminiscent of maternal devotion when he sees the opposite. The love and the protection of women men learned over millions of years crawls away toward extinction.

Men today are less able to provide for their family. They are abandoning the home and returning to the life of a nomad. Children raise themselves without parents, homes crumble, and civilization retrogresses.

5. Sharing the world's goods; right human relations

If a family receives one income versus some two and others zero, every family can meet basic needs and together build a strong community. The middle class developed needed muscle to hold together a society. If split into rich and poor, we essentially have owners and slaves. When a small group of owners seize all power, we enter a totalitarian state.

Reasons Why Woman Should Have a Career

There opens increased opportunities for our children.

If my son or daughter gets beat up every day, I'd work to move to a better neighborhood. Extra money means a choice of better schools, an elevated lifestyle, and more exposure to higher culture.

A woman may find a cure for cancer or make other contributions. We see a higher probability of success when a man and woman work together on a solution.

Woman can and have contributed to mankind through a career.

Any Solution?

Women stand as equals. They should have the same opportunities as man: social, intellectual, and spiritual.

Women differ in every way. They have babies. They have maternal love. Men don't. We are both forced by nature, by design, into different roles.

Although equal often means "the same," it appears physically obvious that the sexes are not the same. Just look! The definition making sense depends on the application; true here, not true there.

Biologically, we both breathe and our hearts pump blood. Then come differences in the body design; the architects can reuse some chemical reactions and must modify others dependent on the sex.

Mentally, we approach situations differently: by sex, by personality.

We keep selling off pieces of the spiritual torch handed down for centuries from mother to son and mother to daughter. We make good money, celebrate family, get together on occasions, and still say grace, but with our best friend, God, we break that connection.

Suppose the world actually gets worse rather than better and we somehow become aware of it. Imagine if politicians and actresses return scientific postulates to scientists and reach the politically incorrect answer that a mother needs to stay at home with children for at least the first five years for civility not to end. What will we do?

Pulling in two salaries only raised the bar on the greed gauge. The promise of computers cutting down our workweek proved a lie. Like a net with a hole, many things that we hoped to keep pass through. It takes more to survive; we only succeeded in upping the mark on greed two notches.

We concur with T. S. Eliot asking why we forfeit our knowledge, wisdom, and even spiritual life for something less worthy. We have data about what toothpaste to buy but don't know if the hygienist picking at our teeth causes cavities or prevents them. Everyone must get a college degree, but we don't know how to change a tire or if our kids need us at home full time or just two hours in the evening. Why do we live?

If philosophers report mankind's pulse, please note the existentialists deem us dead. We contracted cancer of the Spirit. We don't like the diagnosis, so we look for a different doctor. We have the cure in our medicine cabinet but don't bother digesting it. To give man insight into himself and better understand his condition motivates the philosopher to search for truth. The existentialists correctly diagnosed our disease.

The Spirit offers us life and truth. As we change, we change society.

Our careers need to be more flexible.

Married women should receive salaries for staying at home and caring for their children for the first five years. Men should be allocated time to be more involved with their children for the next five years. Both parents should be allowed to commit this order in their lives: (1) God, (2) family, and (3) career.

A society grows only as strong as its marriages, our highest evolutionary accomplishment. The founding of the home lays the foundation for the building blocks of culture and forming altruistic relationships. Even primitive families recognized the home as the best place for the reception of children.

In the distant future, cooperation will replace competition in the work world. We battle in survival mode, and moving up keeps us in meals. I'm up to my waist in mire and having trouble visualizing anything except a slow and painful dissolution of civilization, until it gets so bad that we then focus on securing successful marriages and strong family units and we reconstruct from basic building blocks a society worth living in.

My mother stayed at home to raise me. I consider this my greatest gift that enabled me to appreciate all the ensuing divine gifts from my Heavenly Parents.

The Holy Spirit lives as our spiritual mother here on earth who takes care of all our spiritual needs and promises to always stay at home and watch over us.

Conclusion

Nature sides with men in careers. Women's lives get interrupted with a baby.

When women think only of themselves, conception leads to abortion. When considering the baby, women face a difficult personal, moral, and financial commitment. When any of these fail to be met, we face a "partial" abortion where finding daily care tends toward a loss of caring, moral instruction, and money. A child costs lots of money up front, and for a minimum of thirteen years, this major consumer earns no paycheck.

I agree with Nietzsche. If we ask society to take care of a child, society should have a say. "Thou shalt cease to procreate" strikes me as a more responsible morality than does "Don't worry about having many children."

Time, even in millennia, does not guarantee progress. We assume that after two thousand years the family evolves stronger. The families of the Jewish people who raised Jesus stand far superior to our present-day households.

The "progress" of the Roman Empire ended up as its undoing.

We speed through an anti-Christian route. We turn blind to abortions, like those who didn't bother inquiring where the cattle cars filled with Jews and others were headed. Financial considerations combined with not caring about someone else's life nourish this soil that can only grow weeds.

Careers don't trump kids. If we stood up for children, American companies would back off. Europeans have always demanded a balance.

How woman can have careers and care for children calls for an answer. We need to admit that our present family fails to raise children who are confident that they are watched over and attended to twenty-four hours a day. They hardly know God. Our family's foundation turns out to be sand.

10

Am I Saved?

A simple-enough question. It appears as if there are two answers: yes and no. It may be there are two questions: Am I saved? And will I continue to be saved?

We don't seem to know for sure about ourselves but are fairly confident certain others will not survive.

We are told not to judge others. We don't know their natures or their inner thoughts. We fail, incapable of knowing their heart, will, or soul. We struggle, totally blanketed by pride when judging ourselves, blind as our ego. Only God can judge us righteously.

Sometimes, it sounds easy: the Father wishes all to be saved; the Son came to save all those who are lost; if I have faith, even a small flicker; if I just desire to participate in what God has planned for me.

Sometimes, it sounds difficult: go through the narrow door; it is easier for a camel to pass through the eye of a needle than for a rich (self-satisfied) man; if the tree does not bear fruit, cut it down and toss it into the fire; there are many who will say, "Lord, Lord," and I will answer, "I do not know you"; I know my sheep, and mine know me; unless you become like a little child, you will not enter the kingdom of heaven.

What to Do

Those who take their religion very seriously, the many entering the religious life, want to be assured they survive. Recognizing this as a life-or-death question of survival for eternity or not, they do and should place God as their number one priority.

Like Dostoevsky, who endured a mock execution by the Communists, they begin to live every day as if it were their last. That, essentially, set in motion the existential movement. That provided the key question we should ask ourselves every day: how should I live if this were my last day, even my last second, on earth? For we know not the day or the hour.

Jesus advised us to go through the narrow door, to seek first the kingdom of heaven. Answer the essential question. Go sell everything we own to assure survival. Sacrifice anything to make sure we own a home in the kingdom of heaven.

Though man's survival falls under Not Probable, Jesus's caveat that for God all things become possible comforts us.

If we keep the commandments and love our neighbor as ourselves, but what is love? Our definitions run the gamut from "I decided not to kill him" to "I helped pay his hospital bills." Without love, we have nothing—an empty gong. Defining love can be very subjective.

If Nicodemus doesn't receive a golden rating, then we don't have a prayer. He helps everyone. He spends hours volunteering to help the community. He stands out as a religious leader citing scripture. He never misses church. We honor him as a wonderful family man.

Jesus tells him he stands outside the kingdom of heaven.

The story about Nicodemus scares me. It says good people don't survive. We can help others. We can volunteer to coach our daughter's soccer team. We can go to church daily. No guarantee of survival.

Kierkegaard explained about the ethical man, the modern Nicodemus. He distinguished ethical acts from religious by a "leap of faith"—heart, mind, emotions, and soul; in short, everything—in order to live for Christ. Leave objectivity and all that reasoning behind, and jump. We must leap through heaven's door. Jesus is the way, as he said, and nothing must stand between us and him. Our one goal should be to be like Jesus, and that will take a courageous leap of faith.

We must pause and, like a little child, accept the gift of sonship with God. Our Heavenly Father hands us the kingdom of heaven. What's that wrapped gift that's been sitting there for fifty years? That contains the key to eternity. We have to want to open it. We can't just stand smugly at the door, writing down all our impressive credentials. Rather, discern that someday we will die, and then we ran out of time.

Entry waits for us like an unwrapped gift. We make progress through our efforts in liaison with God. I don't want to stand at judgment empty-handed. If I've shown no interest for an entire lifetime, chances are I don't care about God's kingdom.

So, Do What?

So I do nothing and get into heaven? I dedicate my life to the church, join every committee, help every charity, clock in hours at hunger centers, attend daily Mass, and it's not good enough because I'm not "spiritual"? Should I view the father as lax, making every excuse in the book to save his kid, or a by-the-book judge willing to see his own kid fry?

We portray God as a just judge willing to extend mercy. As soon as I use the word *judge*, I lose the image of a father. I don't judge my children. But I do assess their fitness. I'm constantly worried they'll fit in with friends, that they can play and accept victory and defeat, that they're prepared for most anything, and that they'll do well on their job interview. I know them well enough to honestly assess them.

I think that depicts more what the Father does with us, perfectly and mercifully. An honest assessment connotes different images than a judgment. In a normal relationship, one I shared with my dad, there was never a separation, a denial of sonship. He was stuck with me, and he liked it that, that was the way it is. Sure, there were times he was disappointed. That felt so lousy that I immediately tried to rectify the situation.

So we know the answer. It should be simple. Fathers love their children and would die for their children. Children want to spend as much time as possible with their dads. Children cannot imagine living without their dad. They are with him now, and want to be with him forever.

We complicate a simple and basic relationship. We get too busy. We have other interests. If you don't see your dad for sixty years and one day are forced to be with him, he may truthfully remark, "I don't know you."

Only we can screw up a perfect relationship. Our dad always wants us close to him. If we show no interest in this bond, why would we suddenly want lodging in our Father's house at judgment?

Any group of jurors, especially those in God's court, would sense insincerity.

The question "Am I saved?" reflects selfishness. We serve God and really deserve nothing.

Those who do God's will in their lives rarely think about survival. They're too involved in the family's good works. They fully trust our dad. They've already survived. Death comes round as a formality, like changing clothes.

A parent would rather die than to see their children suffer.

Since our parents are God, we can trust in their care. We will hear "This is the way" on the whole pathway from life on earth to the distant embrace of God, our Father.

Conclusion

Did you hear the good news that we are sons of God? Have you thought about it and dare to believe it? This ennobling truth changes everything. God wants a relationship with us as a friend, as a brother, as a father, and that makes up all that matters.

Do you care how Dad's doing? Do you go see your Brother? Then you know how they feel about you and know you have nothing to worry about.

11

Religious versus Spiritual

I always assumed no difference exists. If I obey my church, follow my religious traditions, I will become a spiritual person.

A few experiences contradicted this, and at an early age.

What an adult considers trivial can impact a child.

I don't remember much of PSR in grade school. I do remember making a crib out of scrap plywood. My mother and father, impressed with my work, told me to take it to PSR and show the nuns.

I brought my cradle to class. The nun smiled and grabbed me by the hand and led me out of the room. I felt apprehensive since being taken out of class usually betokens something not good but calmed myself, thinking I've done nothing wrong. It surprised me how smooth the nun's hands were and that she had no intention of letting go of my hand.

We went to a room, and she told me that my gift to the poor comes greatly appreciated. That ran askew to the reason why I brought my crib in. In fact, I foresaw it shown off as a centerpiece in my living room on the blond coffee table, or at least on the smaller ones by the furnace ducts that we used to lie under when the heat clicked on in winter. I could tell my mother was thinking the same when I first showed it to her.

I felt disappointed, especially when I got home and Mom asked where my cradle was.

Then the nicest neighbor I ever met shocked me.

My mother, who was always kind, asked me to deliver some sweet watermelon to an older woman living down our alley. This elderly woman treated me like she did my mother, and that stood out. She gave me milk instead of coffee, a dessert, and, most important, conversed with me and showed interest in what I was saying.

I found out she did not go to my church. I found out she did not go to *any* church. How could she be such a loving person?

In high school, I got my answer. Soren Kierkegaard explained the difference between religious and spiritual: one whose concern focuses on ethics and one whose concern centers on Christ. We can stay in the ethical stage our entire life.

Using ethics, we could make some bad decisions. Ethical reasoning of the mind can lead one astray. Observe two examples:

We have the Word of God. Nothing can be added or changed. Alterations are the works of Satan. A man with a campaign to change our religion and then blasphemously state he is the 'Son of God' needs to be stopped any way we can. He could mislead the minds of unschooled followers of our one true religion. Besides, we all know he puts on his pants the same as us. (The religious leader's argument against Jesus.)

With tensions running high, I could have had a revolt on my hands and many people killed. Allowing one nobody to be put to death to prevent a bloody riot and loss of countless lives surely constitutes the greater good, or at least the lesser of two evils. Executives have to make the tough decisions. (Pilate allows the death of Jesus).

If we know Christ, we often know the difference between a religious and spiritual person when we meet them. We discern a motive of deep love for Jesus that overrides their human nature, coupled with a sincere concern for the other person. Some concentrate on us and forget their own situation of often far more critical problems.

This analogy occurred to me: becoming an expert in grammar to becoming another Shakespeare. Shakespeare follows the rules of grammar and may break them to reach greater beauty, a work with a spiritual quality.

Kierkegaard calls this a "leap of faith." When relying on faith alone, we would live differently than merely obeying rules set down for us. Nietzsche calls this "going beyond good and evil" to advance over man, to become something better than man.

Jesus spoke to the Jews, a very religious people, that if they only had the faith of a mustard seed, they could accomplish great things.

Eastern religion teaches about the sixth initiation, where we become a master. Churches try to emulate the qualities of saints.

Knowing what spirituality consists of and achieving it lay worlds apart. It begins with an understanding of the differentiation between being religious and being spiritual. It recognizes that a person far more spiritual than you may not go to church.

Jesus did not emphasize going to church. Indeed, the church wanted him dead. The places we find him worshipping and where the spiritual events occurred were outside in nature: at a river, on a mountain, or in a garden.

In marriage, we find making love easy but living love taking effort. Sex provides a key ingredient but hardly makes up the whole formula.

How do we teach someone to love? How can I love every day? How do I love more? It bodes of a long road but one that Jesus travelled. He willed to do the good. He daily sought to communicate with his Father and to do his Father's will, namely implementing good works. He always behaved like God's son would, and he accomplished this as a human and not by simply actually being God's Son. He read the scriptures. He experienced the problems of an ordinary existence one day at a time, ever putting his trust in his Heavenly Dad.

The direction we're headed when we die matters. I will never be as loving or talented as many others, but someday, I will. I know because my compass points that way.

The Universe Is Good

Father Leahy delivered one sermon I've never forgotten. He believed if you can't get your point across in three minutes, you've lost your audience. God bless Father Leahy!

Father Leahy held a white cardboard placard and asked, "What do you see?" Our answers were "Nothing" and "A blank sheet." He then drew a tiny black dot in the center and again asked. We responded, "A black dot."

"Anything else?"

"No," we assured him.

"Now we see the purpose of the Holy Spirit: to help us see the large white area of our soul when we concentrate only on the small black dot."

The universe also compares to a large white sheet, with isolated sin showing up like small black dots. It helps to remember that the entire universe shines bright and the few dots will someday disappear. We struggle to visualize a good and organized universe while here on earth. If the news reported all the amazing things people do in their daily lives, the small and large kindness, the coming home from work, and the hugging of our children, perhaps the phenomenon of evil would look more like what it is: temporary and an anomaly.

Jesus wants spiritual children, not religious children.

He summed up the 613 ethical laws of the Pharisees into "Love God and neighbor." He challenged his apostles to "love as I have loved you."

Jesus did not enter the priesthood of the time. He had hoped that he could win them over to his message. Their crystallizing of truth in their religion stopped them from embracing the spiritual freedom Jesus offers.

Jesus remained obedient to the rules of the temple and followed civil laws. He assumed people were ethical.

That's why he choose to be born a Jew, the most moral and God-seeking people in the world. Yet those unwilling to transition from the religious to the spiritual killed Jesus.

It takes God's help for us to transition from the fear of God with rules, breaking rules, consequences, and then forgiveness, to a love of God: I'm loved and don't want to do anything to betray that love.

We're not in a courtroom. We're in a family.

Conclusion

A religious man may be spiritual. A spiritual man may be religious. Only when a religious man fails to become spiritual do hypocrisy and trouble follow.

Caiaphas reached the pinnacle of the religious order. When he met Jesus, he did not see anything there that he wanted to become.

Nicodemus reached the pinnacle of a good man. See the neighbor who takes his family to Mass every Sunday, is the city's Volunteer of the Year, is the Little League coach, the man who always supports kids selling stuff for their school? Now tell me one believes the story circulating that he met Jesus and Jesus told him he has yet to enter the kingdom of heaven, that he currently has no survival qualities. Surprised? Then read the Bible story about Nicodemus.

The good, ethical man, the religious man, does not survive death. The spiritual man does. That constitutes a big difference.

We wrestle, being incapable of becoming spiritual. We are composed of dust, and unto dust our bodies return. Spirit comes into us as a gift from God. The divine fragment comes down and dwells in every normal human mind. This spiritual gift of God the Father within us desires to make us spiritual, to form our soul, to be born again within.

Nicodemus sought out Jesus and was born again. He became a follower of Jesus and may invite us over for a few libations when we too pass from this world.

12

Jesus Ain't Jesus

Jesus Does Not Advocate Socialism

We believe the vision of Jesus for our world demands a generous sharing of goods.

Does that make Jesus a socialist?

Communism claims to be based on socialism, which claims to share all goods.

Does that make Jesus a communist?

Communism wants Jesus dead. Their leaders declare Christianity a crime and reeducates any believer, meaning being sequestered into harsh conditions until dead.

Communism, in practice, relies on a totalitarian government that uses cruelty and separateness. The few in power stand against all the rest to maintain the few in power. Socialism allows them to divide one man's million dollars with a million people, so all have one dollar. No money, no power, dependent on the government: perfect for maintaining power. Those "equal" quickly learn some are more equal than others.

Jesus does not advocate socialism, and Communism stands against everything he taught.

Didn't Jesus advocate an equal sharing of goods? This was certainly the (mis)understanding of the early Christian community who shared a commune thinking, where all possessions were turned over to the common good. The poor benefited for a very short period, and the wealthy became indigent. They could not provide for themselves or their families and soon became beggars.

This flawed thinking derives from the young centurion who desired to become a disciple of Jesus. Jesus instructed him to go and sell all he had and give the proceeds to the poor. The centurion had been taught that possessions signify a special favor from God. Jesus knew the centurion's love of wealth would stop him from full fellowship with the other ninety disciples who left all to follow Jesus. He would not fit in. Since the centurion believed wealth meant God's blessing, he walked away sad.

Jesus asked the centurion to give up the one thing that was holding him back from full fellowship. We all own that one thing. Jesus never viewed wealth as bad. When it consumes all our time and our success veers toward independence from God, then we need to weigh our gains and losses. Jesus did say wealth includes responsibility, and we will be asked how we used it.

The apostles and disciples lived as one, like a family. They could not afford a shirker among them. They ousted an idle person. When funds dipped, they all returned to their careers to renew the coffers.

The Jews believe in hard work, even to this day. They would often quote, "He who does not work does not eat." Jesus quoted these words too.

Jesus never exhibited pity to the weak or those who gave up. He expected man to make the most of the talents they were given. Alms were never handed out at random. Two apostles, or an apostle and Jesus, had to approve. Jesus taught that indiscriminate kindness causes many social ills. To support a phlegmatic sleepyhead helps as much as handing a wino two dollars, which he uses to purchase cheap wine.

God's idea of brotherhood stands in opposition to forcing his followers to be burdened by indolent people who refuse to work. We are not expected to help every poor person we encounter, let alone in our nation, let alone in the world. To distribute everyone's wealth equally would make everyone poor and destroy any incentive to work. However, a vast disparity also cries out as an injustice.

We need a work program so people can earn a living and better our society. We need everyone employed.

We have limited jobs and limited food. God never intended any man to be a burden on another. God never intended for the man who is working two jobs to feed his family to give half to those out of work. God never intended for people living in a nice house to be thrown out and a poor family moved in. God never intended the people living in a nice house to be blind to those living in squalor.

What we want to think and how we think God wants us to think confuses what we think.

Politicians need to present arguments so they can take more of our finances, gain votes, and portray it as for the better good. They remind us of a television show that engages us even though we cannot remember anything said and certainly would not wish to live as any of the characters, and further steals our time.

Churches demand social justice and pay their lay workers poverty-level salaries.

Jesus wants men to solve problems by thinking clearly.

We send our best to war. We steal from the rich and give to the poor.

Everyone loves Robin Hood. That the king usurped power and exploited the people for self-aggrandizement makes everyone want to see him fall.

But not hardworking families who work tirelessly for the good of their children.

In Ayn Rand's analogy, the creative leaders befit Atlas, who supports the burden of the world and keeps it spinning. We reach the point where the burden outweighs the benefit and is no longer worth the effort; those who don't work make more than some who work. Atlas decides to shrug the world off his shoulders.

In *Robin Hood*, the good men volunteered to go off to war, leaving the bad men to rule. The government took everyone's money, forcing the young men who could not yet join a brother-in-arms to take the money back from the government by breaking the law.

Socialism feigns to be an answer to society's problems and succeeds in securing political power for a few. They target the largest group, the poor, with promises of equality. By convincing them that they are helping, they help themselves by increased votes. Every such leader requires an object of hatred: the Jews for Hitler, Goldstein in *1984*, and the wealthy for socialists. For staying in power, socialism destroys any incentive to do anything, to be anything, or to take action to overthrow those in power.

Socialism attracts as a theory with what sounds like equal sharing. Making everyone equal simplifies the task for someone wanting to take over, and that someone never turns out to be someone good.

Where we find more people than food, more people than jobs, we learn that civilization ends at the refrigerator door. People kill for food.

Civilization turns a savage into a scientist and encourages his better self in place of his worse.

We have increased our yield from the soil. We have invented means to harvest and transport produce fresh to market. We have not controlled the number of mouths to feed.

We recoil, afraid of telling someone that they cannot have as many children as they want. But we must to prevent starvation, hatred, and war.

Don't Give to the Poor?

The church honors those who give everything to the poor, especially if they become poor themselves. They declare them saints and recommend we emulate them. Elizabeth of Hungary's royal family tossed her out after she gave away the family's treasures to the poor. Mother Teresa received worldwide recognition for working with people who owned nothing, including food.

The church provides many programs that help the poor. Students of secular institutions, hoping for scholarships, must provide mucho service hours to the community, especially in hunger centers and clothing drives. The church recently voiced out that everyone must be entitled to proper health care.

The sharing of wealth becomes expected. We assume the giving away of riches as always honorable. The sharing of all goods makes for a better world. For lack of a more neutral term, socialism should be embraced by Christians.

This falsehood continues to fool many.

A Christian's first responsibility on earth requires him to use his talents and become a productive member of society: to get a job. Unfortunately, we often encounter a mismatch of a person's skill set with job opportunities—another problem we are expected to solve.

Once successful in securing employment, spending time and talents for others should follow, as Jesus did after he saw to the needs of his family.

Jesus paid taxes and church fees. He obeyed laws and stayed away from man's evolutionary development of social service, economics, and politics.

Jesus disapproved of a greedy businessman as much as an unmotivated indigent who wastes his abilities.

The hard worker who falls into difficult times needs our helping hand. The irresponsible person who continues to have children and feels entitled by the government and the church that because we hold life precious that society must provide for his babies reflects not at all what Jesus taught, and is only allowed by poor governance that needs to be replaced.

Jesus Does Not Hate the Rich nor Favor the Poor

Jesus did not view poverty as a virtue. The poor, whose schedules were usually wide open, could afford the time to hear about Jesus. They did not pile up accomplishments as those who worked hard for a position. We take pride in our hard work, and the glory and source of our gifts belong to God. When we gather self-sufficiency and believe we owe nothing to God, then we close our ears to God's Word. God welcomes the humble executive. God welcomes the willing-to-trust poor. Jesus enrolls more of the poor.

"Blessed are the poor in spirit" means those who know that without Christ, they are nothing. "Blessed are the poor" makes little sense other than they have fewer evasions to keep from listening.

The poor having preference before God reduces largely as envy of those who are successful. We shield our satisfaction when Richard Cory shoots himself. We are dissatisfied with our station, and the rich owner takes more of the profits, so we wish him ill.

We should pray that the wealthy discern that they will need to answer for how they used their wealth. Richard Cory worked hard, deserved his position, and became someone to emulate. How tragic it was that somewhere inside grew emptiness that he did not know how to fill.

No one earns a special standing before God. Rich or poor, Jew or Gentile, God treats all the same. Death comes to all. Our work résumé dies with us. God knows every person as an individual, alone and standing before God.

The Jews showed a greater interest in God than any other race and were chosen for the incarnation of Jesus. After centuries of searching for God, the closest they came was "I am who am"—God eternal. The race largely rejected Jesus and continues to do so. Their own belief of touting themselves as a chosen race contains more ego than fact.

Jesus Does Not Think We Are Equal

This world contains far more inequalities.

Consequently, almost every system of thought identifies classifications as lesser to greater. Educational psychologists identify advancing stages from rote memory to creative deductions. Psychologists discuss a selfish personality contrasted to a compassionate person who looks beyond their own needs. Philosophers speak of the beast (Nietzsche's term) or aesthetic (Kierkegaard's term) to the overman ("over" man) or spiritual person.

America's founders crafted the principle that all men are created equal under law. They dropped off the last two words. To John Adams, the statement made little sense without the "under law."

Jesus loves all men equally. God makes only two distinctions: those who follow his will and those who don't. Differences in spirituality become more obvious in our next life; we see one's soul.

Not being able to see one's soul on earth makes determining someone's intentions difficult. We glean evidence from behavior; by the fruit, we know the tree.

Discrimination—differential treatment—remains our best tool for survival and progress.

We apply it every day. If I go through a red light, I get an expensive ticket. Schools give grades. We administer national tests to help colleges rank potential students. Other criteria play in, but the attainment of knowledge helps determine the ability to do well in college, and it proves folly to ignore relevant factors.

I'd give preferential treatment to anyone in the armed forces. Open jobs up, and hire them as an experienced candidate. Given the hostility in much of the world, every eighteen-year-old should serve one year in the armed forces. Anyone who serves his nation, willing to give his life for others, understands public service far more than those who never served. Use credentials, service, and experience to recommend hiring and promotions.

We have two confused ideas that warp our application of discrimination:

1. The concept of equal rights.

    We fight for even the right to breathe. Many possess no rights. A few evolved a government where we collectively pay for security: defense, police protection, and putting out fires. We have the right to expect benefits from what we pay for.

    Lucifer made self-assertion his battle cry. When we demand personal rights, do what works best for us, and place ourselves above law, we adopt the thinking of Lucifer. On the contrary, mature citizens surrender some of their own freedom to live together with others. The

Gregg Tomusko

development of law signals how far a culture has advanced.

Why does being equal have so much appeal? The ideal that we are given equal opportunity ignites our hope. I can actually be something if I put my mind to it. I just empowered myself and implanted a goal. We unearth enough goodness in those living Christian lives that they truly want everyone to be able to work toward and to realize their dream. We become individuals, responsible for our own success. This ideal brings out the best in us.

What ruins any good idea? We introduce lies, cheating, and greed. Some warp the concept for gain.

"Equal rights" grows confusing quickly. Everyone should be allowed to take photos; some inspire us by capturing flowers that color a mountainside, and some imprison us by showing children in suggestive poses. Everyone can go to a museum; some are moved emotionally by a Van Gogh, and some move the painting under cover of their overcoat.

In the presixties, below are the bases of how we discriminated

- Preference to the military
- Male supporting a family; female supporting herself
- Experience; having done the job before
- Education; college degree versus high school

146

After the Cultural Revolution, this is how we now discriminate

- Based on sex; female over male
- Based on race; minority preferred
- Experience in doing whatever it takes
- Education; college degree if willing to take a low salary
- Preference to the nonmilitary

We can debate the order, especially from individual experience. The motive changed from striving to be objective and finding the best candidate into a desire to look liberal and support a political cause introduced by the sixties' Cultural Revolution.

Nietzsche exposed several deep-rooted ideas as sheer stupidity on our part and as a means to destroy anything successful. He tried to uproot the seeds planted by Lucifer that especially appealed to an opportunist rash enough to give themselves absolute power. He detested Hitler.

I interviewed for a teaching position in the suburbs. The principal and I shared similar backgrounds, and he commented I placed as the best candidate for the job. Off the record, he told me he had to hire a woman or a minority. I figured I didn't have to put up with such nonsense, so I left teaching and went into business.

Business needs to make a profit, or it ceases to exist. They could hardly afford to take this approach.

Turns out, it only took a few more years. Our corporate goal hoped to achieve 70 percent of management to be women. Women got promoted then mentored by upper management so they can be handed higher positions.

The man across from me works close to sixty hours a week and is on call 24-7. The woman across comes and goes as she pleases and works from home every Friday. The gentleman they let go. He died of bone cancer shortly after. The woman socializes, receives education during work hours and challenging assignments that she offloads for others to do and then explain to her, and enjoys increases in salary.

Having different rules, playing favorites reoccur as the mistakes of a first-year teacher whom no one likes or respects. Naturally a business blatantly run like this allows the favored to take full advantage of their myopic vision. I no longer refer to this company as a business but rather as a liberal's experiment. Imagine in baseball benching the top athletes because the less talented play less games. We defend this under equal rights and call out the best players making the team as unfair.

Nietzsche saw through the demand for equal rights and thought it could undo a civilization. It gives life a gloomy and questionable aspect. I can see what he means.

2. Jesus does not hold us responsible for our ancestors.

   We bear no responsibility for the sins of our ancestors whether real or made up. When mythical, we employ the less-precise term *perception* to substantiate lying.

   Not understanding infirmities, people would ask Jesus, "Which ancestor sinned, since this man is blind?" Jesus explained that sin does not cause blindness. Further, God does not approve of such crass justice as to hold a man responsible for anything his ancestors did.

   Jesus encouraged man to research and discover a cure. Since science offered the spittle of a holy man mixed with mud as the best remedy of the time, Jesus applied the mixture to the man's eyes then told him to show himself to the priests. While knowing dirt and spit prove totally ineffective as a cure, Jesus restored the eyesight. Whether Jesus accomplished this as a miraculous cure or at his command spiritual beings applied advanced science to fix the eyeball, I do not know. I do know that Jesus did this partially to encourage us to find physical cures. He also wanted to challenge the religious leaders by utilizing their own belief that the spittle of a holy man always proves efficacious and that this would open their eyes to who Jesus was.

Jesus Walks Away from People Who Live in Sin

Jesus behaves differently toward sinners as those with sincere hearts.

He goes out to look for the lost sheep who have been misled and not those rebellious wolves that willingly kill.

Jesus did not even acknowledge the murderer about to be crucified. The thief was fooled into seeing Barabbas as a hero because he used violence as a patriotic protest and political tool but realized his mistake when he looked upon Jesus. He then understood what being a true hero meant. Jesus brought him words of everlasting life.

Jesus refused to talk to Caiaphas or Herod. He answered Pilate only when Pilate showed an interest in knowing the truth. Jesus advised his apostles to never cast pearls before swine. When the multitude turned unfriendly, Jesus taught in parables to confuse the undiscerning and insincere while still imparting words from heaven to those who wanted to listen.

We welcome people who live in sin. We are taught to not judge, to suppress our morals.

We believe everyone looks precious in the eyes of God. God doesn't make garbage because deep within shines a diamond, our immortal soul. We are obligated to get sinners to see the light up to the moment they pass from this world. Why then did God not bother?

Our Immortal Soul

We believe God gave man an immortal soul. If the soul lives forever, then after death it must exist someplace. It follows the content of goodness would determine its destination, so we need good, bad, and in-between, or heaven, hell, and purgatory.

The soul forms and grows from two factors: the material contribution of the good we do in our lives and the spiritual posting of that good by our spiritual advisor, an actual spiritual fragment of God the Father that dwells in all normal minds. This spirit encourages us and adjusts our thinking to help us attain survival qualities. A living, immortal soul forms and shines brighter with each decision we willingly make in line with God's thinking.

When ice heats, we produce water, with very different properties. Add more heat, and we get steam. We hardly recognize the same compound, H2O, in ice and steam. Heat makes them very different. In a similar way, matter and spirit meet halfway as a substance not found on our periodic chart and is not spirit. Our next body will be of this substance, and our souls will be visible to one another. Yet it is hardly physical matter and not spirit.

This enterprise that we call the soul survives death. God and man form a partnership in our Father's business intended to last forever and grow ever stronger, ever brighter.

Free will forbids one to be forced into a partnership, not even one with God. Not every company survives.

When someone decides they want nothing to do with God and embrace evil, that person chooses spiritual death. He or she may be alive physically on earth, busy killing others, but once the Spirit adjudges the person as morally bankrupt, the spirit fragment departs and takes any experience worth registering with it. The soul ceases to exist, the total valuation returned to the Spirit. The mortal awaits only physical death, much like a lightbulb that burns out and gives no light, yet the circuit continues to carry electricity. Despite the temporary continuation of living energies, the man functions merely as an intricate computer.

Some contribute nothing, bearing no fruit, snuffing out the spark. The immortal soul can return nothing to the Spirit that created it. The person ceases to exist spiritually, the opposite of what the Father had hoped for. God the Father figuratively buries his child whom he loved.

Others embark on an eternal career full of fun and adventure and learning. As we become more perfect and spiritual, we reach the decision to fuse our soul with the divine spirit guide within, our longtime friend. We call this permanent change substantial in cosmology. It cannot be undone. We have started down the road of becoming a spirit and being perfect.

Jesus came to call sinners and welcome them back to his embrace. Some refuse, and he honors their will and never coerces them.

Since sin cannot be an aspect of God, he necessarily stands at a distance. God views evil as antireality in the sense that it contains the seeds of its own destruction. The wages of sin lead to death, where death means nonexistence beyond this first brief life.

Sin and Evolving Man

As man evolves, his understanding of the nature of sin also advances as he glimpses better into the true nature of sin.

We cannot judge the past using present standards, especially if they swerved as more misguided and judgmental. Evolution allows the smarter and healthier to survive. Stronger tribes exterminated less prepared groups—every man, woman, and child—allowing generations of "better survivors." Societies made a conscious effort to procreate only those with physical ability and mental alertness; those with deformities died. As treaties and government evolved, the finest man and woman would mate. This also helped amalgamate the races.

The divine plan includes evolution, assuring the survival of the best qualities, blending the diverse genetic combinations, and resulting in one race and one language. For early man, the animal instincts aided this, with later man's intelligence guided by superb instructors as Lucifer, Satan, and, later, Adam and Eve. It's very unusual for a planet not to venerate such teachers and hold them forever in esteem.

The key to getting through college relies on having good professors. They will either make or break your success. I walked into a class and did not understand anything the teacher said. When I realized that I saw all this information in the prerequisite I had just aced but was now explained so poorly I didn't even recognize the material, I dropped the class on day one.

Many of our spiritual teachers left us confused. Suggesting the barbarism of early man unfolded as part of God's plan at that time, as natural as a cougar taking down a yearling, certainly rates as novel teaching. Who thinks of slavery as an evolutionary advancement?

Rather than mutilate everything still breathing, which sums most conquerors, we exploited the vanquished as manual labor. Those good at working the land were more likely to stay alive. We now see slavery more clearly— as an exploitive practice—but back then, it marked an evolutionary triumph.

Jesus, a great teacher, ever challenged his students. We can contemplate on every word he spoke, and the more we meditate on their meaning, the more profound they become.

We arrive at different interpretations in our attempts to fully understand. Jesus upgraded our comprehension of God and stated that his words were meant for all time. Future generations will have a clearer idea of what he said.

I'm sure it upset Jesus to see many abuses and exploitations during his lifetime. He rarely commented on them, and many remain prevalent today. He stayed true to his task: to uplift people spiritually and then let that spirit-led person solve the problems encountered every day in society, national government, and world economics.

Jesus Does Not Solve Political, Economic, or Social Problems

Jesus made this our job. Jesus teaches us to seek first the kingdom of God, establish ourselves there, and then we become the best man for any job. Spirit-led persons should figure out the most lasting solutions to problems. Many despair over problems that seem overwhelming and continue to get worse. Fast solutions for personal gain aggravate the problem. Political solutions to secure votes augment the problem, like watching your eyeglasses pulled off by a wave and disappear in the ocean: you can't see, and you can't drive home.

Many at least think about what could be done and try to improve the quality of life around them. Often the slow and patient way that Jesus employed, stopping to help one individual at a time, makes a lasting change. Spiritual advancements come first, and that results in the up-stepping of all other endeavors of mankind. Once convinced of the righteousness of a goal, like filling up the car with gas, we stand ready to go!

Jesus Is Not Politically Correct

Jesus addressed his opponents as "liars, hypocrites, and blind guides." When we care about a person and want to save their souls, we talk straightforward, time-to-wake-up truth. Jesus did not cower before the powerful religious leaders. They were in the wrong and about to commit a murderous act. He didn't apologize for all the good he did and didn't suggest that he could have waited until after the Sabbath to perform some of his cures so he could find common ground with his enemies. He warned them of their folly and the seriousness of what they planned to do. Jesus would not compromise his position of truth and doing good.

Words can cut deep. A poem stays with me about a little girl—innocent and seeing the world as an exciting adventure—cut down as if by a machine gun from someone calling her a hate-filled term. Such cruel and thoughtless connotations devastate. I heard *nigger* often and quite unexpectedly while teaching in the inner city. Blacks calling another this word meant "Act right."

A human tongue, like a gun, can be used to save someone or destroy them.

The Pharisees regarded Jesus as an anarchist and believed it their duty to prevent him from corrupting others, and so they had him murdered. There appears a way that seems right to a man but leads to his spiritual death. We still fill boatloads, drifting like blocks of wood down a river and lost out to sea. Few jump off—alone, as an individual—and swim to shore.

Jesus Does Not Celebrate Multicultures

Babel towers as a doomed culture because its citizens spoke multiple languages. Babies babble, only concerned about their needs. *Babble* and *baby* sound like Babel, which derives from an ancient Hebrew word that means "confusion of speech." As in the Bible, the children of men continue to "reach unto heaven; and let us make us a name," building models of diversity.

There will be no peace on earth until we speak one language. By speaking different tongues, we assure a lack of trust, a primary requisite to love.

We face an added burden to have multiple races and countless languages. It continues to be more difficult to get along. It also takes a spiritual person to see all people as having one spiritual father and see all men as brothers. Although a tall order, those able to achieve this viewpoint stand mighty in the kingdom of God. They earn advanced credentials in this and in the next world.

Jesus Is Not a Spaced Wimp

We mistakenly portray Jesus.

He developed into a hardy and muscular laborer. He worked every day and travelled long distances on foot. He could beat the crap out of you.

He evicted the money changers from the temple. Tough fisherman called him their master.

The scrawny, skinny man from the movies ain't Jesus.

His words evinced power. We can meditate on them every minute of our lives and not exhaust their meaning.

The illusion of finding great wisdom in the life of an alcoholic, drifter, or drug user usually ends up as not the best source. Jesus drawling diminutive syllables to form sentences that don't follow one another while staring vacuously in an apparent semiconscious state ain't Jesus. He commanded everyone's attention as a bold and enthusiastic speaker. Nothing ever stood in the way of his portrayal of how wonderful his Father was.

Jesus feared no man. He stood calm when on trial for his life, knowing that actually Pilate stood on trial.

Jesus faced death unafraid. His only concern revolved around the safety of his apostles. He worried about others and not himself even when his life raced toward a terrible ending.

Reading about a person reveals far less than meeting them in the flesh and conversing, where a personal reaction forms entirely unique to me. Others may form a completely different impression.

Many wish they could have met Jesus in the flesh and talked with him about their lives and problems. How blessed are the eyes of the apostles to be able to see Jesus here on earth. We have to wait but then before long will sup with Jesus and notice certain manners and whims and facial expressions that we can only know once we actually sit down with him.

Projecting the advances in media, perhaps in our next life we'll be able to view the life of Jesus back on earth as if it were actually occurring real time.

Jesus wants to become our best friend. That's why he poured out his Spirit upon the earth to always be available. The Father wants to be intimate with us and so sent part of his Spirit to dwell in our minds. God longs to spend every minute with us, like the bond of marriage where two become as one, only closer.

Conclusion

Jesus won't be popular for a long time. He says a lot of things we don't want to hear. Yet everyone thinks he's on their side.

His teachings concern spiritual matters. If we apply the words of Jesus to social, economic, or political realms, they don't translate. He never spoke on these matters and does not today. These are problems he expects humans to solve, albeit spiritual men should find the most lasting solutions.

Jesus came from a line of achievers. They believed in hard work and diligent study. They made the most of their situation and took care of their family first. Jesus's ministry he delayed until when in his late twenties because his family needs had to be met. This falls not contrary to the Father's will; this embraces his Father's will.

"If we don't work, we don't eat" follows as cause and effect. Jesus wanted those who labor to come to him. When the coffers bottomed out, Jesus required everyone to return to their livelihood. On occasion, Jesus refused to give alms knowing arbitrary charity only causes more problems. He simply passed by some and told his apostles to do the same as to "cast no pearls." He offered no pity to weak, lazy, or dissolute mortals.

13

There's Got to Be a Reason Why the New Age Thrives

The New Age appealed to me. It held "hidden knowledge."

Here lay a whole body of thought that I just discovered. Half the world thinks differently, and I had no idea there even existed another approach.

I met an articulate, intelligent, and humble man who became my teacher. He labored as an esoteric astrologer. He held a new tool to answer spiritual questions such as "Why am I here?" "For what purpose are we here on earth?" and "What career should I go into?" He read a birth chart like a book. His answers were specific and personal.

The New Age answers fundamental questions and on a more personal level. The adage that the ascent of mankind brings about the descent of divinity places emphasis on making man better—right here, right now, on this earth. We learn a lot more about ourselves and appreciate our unique personality.

If something applies directly to me and is so specific it only fits me, of course I'll listen.

Here I present some answers given to me. The first I received from my church's catechism, which I attended once a week as a child to a young adult and which I now teach as an adult; the second was from a two-hour astrology reading as an adult.

Most guys ask their number one concern: "What career?"

Church: We deem all work noble. When offered up to the greater glory of God, toil turns into a holy task.

Esoteric astrology: The teaching profession (that I was in) suits you, but you need harmony, so the inner city may be too rough. Since you have Uranus in your tenth house, computers may be a good fit (which I am now in). Your personality chart shows a desire to make a lot of money, but that is not what your soul wants you to do. If you take that path, you won't feel right or think right, and may become unhealthy since you have Virgo (health) rising. You were in a past life involved in the priestcraft (elevated Jupiter). That you put behind you, and good you're through with it (I studied right out of high school to be a priest). You have to be careful: religious practices you regard as very important, but watch that they don't lead into hypocrisy.

"What is my purpose on earth?"

Church: To love and serve God. The best way is to become a priest.

Esoteric astrology: The path of your soul points to being a teacher, especially on spiritual subjects. You're a second-ray soul (love and wisdom) and a fifth-ray personality (science and technology), and on your third initiation. You must use your mind to influence others. You like reading philosophers and religious thinkers, and your job in this lifetime entails to interpret and teach what you learned. That's why you're interested in this stuff (esoteric astrology).

There are things from your past that need to be resolved this time around. You have a strong link with your mother that will be dissolved soon. See Saturn, the past, conjunct the moon, your mother, with Saturn heading into Neptune, which will dissolve Karma. You know Saturn represents Karma, especially long-standing Karma, and Neptune, the sea. Water dissolves almost anything.

You have an aversion to women here with Venus square Mars. This happens because religion, your elevated Jupiter, sits very strong in you. You don't like this free sex movement and don't want to put yourself in situations where there might be hanky-panky!

There should be a lot of activities, changes, and experiences in your life because you have a T-cross, where energies clash then seek a release in creative outlets ruled by the fifth house.

"What's the soul?"

Church: A gift from God that lives immortal and separates us from the animals.

Esoteric astrology: The natal chart shows your soul. It is the plan configured for you to make maximum spiritual growth. You will be given the opportunity to experience everything you need to learn to make progress. I can see your past lives, what you need to be working on this time around, and future experiences. But first I have to find out where you are spiritually—what initiation you are working on, what ray each of your bodies are. The spirit descends through the multiple planes: spiritual, mental, astral, physical. I will take you to each of these planes and ask your soul to take a form. You are not just the physical you here before me, you are also working on all these other planes.

As I felt myself leaving my body and proceeding to the next plane and asking my soul to take a form, I did sense travelling upward and saw forms. On the third plane—the mind—I observed bright lights shining downward.

I cannot explain it. To this day, forty years later, I still cannot dismiss esoteric studies although as a math and science guy, the energy from heavenly bodies affecting my life personally doesn't sound right. I don't know how this man knew so much about me, some deeply personal. The experience of going to higher planes felt real. The key question again resurfaces: is this true?

I don't know. I studied the "textbook," the works of Alice Bailey (Master DK), but was unable to make sense of it.

I can make only one point. It provides very personal answers to fundamental questions.

There's Got to Be a Reason
Why People Are Leaving the Church

The church has less of Christ and more of social concerns. We can get that anywhere.

In the future, the faith *of* Jesus will be emphasized. Today, we teach a faith in Jesus, along with church doctrine.

A triumphant Christ rising from the grave naturally soared into primary importance for the defeated apostles.

All of Jesus's teachings to his followers suddenly became secondary. His followers started emphasizing Jesus, who rose from the dead.

Jesus had no interest in creating a religion, especially one about him. St. Paul sure wanted to, and did. St. Paul never served as one of Jesus's close companions yet contributed the most to Christian teachings. Much of the preaching and personal emphasis Jesus bestowed upon the twelve apostles ended up lost.

Jesus spoke about the Father. Jesus purposely left no material behind—no writing, and only the clothes off his back. He left only the life he lived here on earth, a life in service to man and out of love for God. Jesus each day centered his faith in the Father. He showed us that when we believe, we should believe as faith-filled sons and daughters of God.

I can't imagine being born and told only that I was God's son. I would guess that I would want to know all I could about my dad. Since the best source would be Jesus, I'd delve into the Gospels. I would probably reflect on my relationship with God throughout the day and want to meet him.

I would certainly be open to any person who also showed an interest in knowing God. I could spot the better ideas presented in many books. I would probably choose a religion that came closest to my understanding. Perhaps I'd worship God whenever and wherever I happen to be.

Would I be closer to God living in the way that Jesus approached religion or by accepting the faith as handed down by my family? In either case, only the burning search for the truth enkindles our heart and keeps us spiritually alive. It would be easier if our parents taught us Jesus's approach when a child. Unfortunately, all too often we're instead simply handed a religion box of completed paperwork that we're asked to read over and memorize.

Christ alive in our individual lives every second and doing all he can to spiritualize our souls conveys the experience of religion. The natural desire to share this wonderful experience with others established the social church.

The church must promote the individual before Christ. The doctrines of the congregation receiving Christ in the Eucharist or the church as Christ's mystical body while profound should not supersede first bringing an individual personally into the real presence of Christ. A gathering of individuals in love with Christ stands distinct from mandatory attendance at a select location, albeit they can work hand in hand.

New Age Is Good

The ancient wisdom survives as a well thought-out theory with origins as old as the Old Testament.

Esoteric astrology can be a great aid to every person. Knowing thyself and thy spiritual purpose could head everyone in the right direction. That we have a soul, one that can manifest itself on the different planes that we can visit, talk to, and see its form, makes this a concrete belief. We discover man's spiritual nature described and experienced in very personal terms. I learn of the work I am meant to do on this planet.

A spiritual government supervises mankind. An ancient adage goes "As above, so below." Here on this planet, invisible spiritual beings help us to progress and make this a better place for everyone.

Every soul that incarnates, a unique and important part of God, plays a key role in the full manifestation of the Supreme. The will of God being established on our planet takes every one of us to accomplish.

We are all evolving. We are all learning. This earth encapsulates a classroom where all the lessons and opportunities to advance were inscribed in the teacher's lesson plan. We expedite our growth when our souls decide to incarnate on earth, like a challenging field trip. Nothing ends up wasted. Everything fulfills some design. It all works out for the good because God commands the enterprise.

Eternal punishment for sin dies with our guarantee to progress. The only hell would be what we go through here on earth. If we create bad karma for ourselves due to our immaturity, we simply reincarnate and try to again learn the same lessons until we get it right, like being able to take the same test over until we pass.

We see all men as brothers. The degenerate that we deemed smart to disassociate from transform into our younger brothers, newer souls that lack the experience we have. We were once like them.

As any good theory, it offers consistency. All souls have a preexistence, and many chose to incarnate. All men, through many incarnations, can become masters. Some return to earth to aid their younger brothers. The better known are Jesus, Buddha, and Mohammad.

I liked the idea of not being forced to do anything. Don't have to go to church. Don't have to worry about sin, no self-examination. Just spend every day trying to help people. I can know many deep-rooted and secret things about people through their astrological charts and be able to guess what spiritual step or initiation their foot rests upon.

New Age Is Bad

Theories come from men, revelation from God. Even the best theories have to state the domain and conditions under which the theory holds true. Yeah, I finally get to use my math! "Analytic over the region except for a finite number of isolated poles [noncontinuous areas]…"

Jesus having a preexistence does not mean man does. God tends to be an exception to every man-made theory. God can even divide by zero!

A favorite puzzle of mine depicts the Last Supper. The last time I put it together, I was missing one piece: the face of Jesus. To Christianity, that's the main piece. To the New Age, missing Peter or Judas would be of equal importance.

Jesus Is God

Only Jesus has a preexistence and could've chosen where to incarnate. We're here because God shares his parental powers with his children. Our parents bring us into existence, and we inherit much of what they got.

The apostles called Jesus master. The Father's spiritual fragment revealed to Peter that Jesus is the Son of God.

This fragment of God reveals this truth to those whom the Father chooses to give it to.

I believe the Gospel words it this way—"The Father chooses"—to show knowledge as a gift. The Father wants to tell everyone this fact if only we're willing to listen.

Jesus as only a man—this stood out as the one discomfort and warning sign that I always questioned about New Age thinking. I appreciate the consistency of stating that many godlike people appeared on earth. So Jesus falls in with the rest as the best of the group?

I doubt that. His words last forever, ripe with eternal meanings and waiting for us to pick them and sink our teeth into. They grow on the tree of life. Would I proclaim "I am the truth, the way, and the life"? "I am the living waters. I am the Son of God"? If I made this claim, it would be blasphemous, besides being utterly ridiculous. I cannot own a rational, normal mind and state such things.

"I am the resurrection and the life." Christ raised Lazarus from the grave and himself rose from among the dead. That tells of the power of God exclusively.

Without a God that I can know as a person, to be able to appreciate his loving and selfless personality and talk to and commune with and delight in his company, all the life-giving joy of falling in love with Jesus disappears. We do not love the New Age god. We appreciate this god as a profound theory but not as a person. If asked to love all the qualities of Buddha and Mohammed and Confucius and Jesus and Moses and all those the New Age deem as masters, it becomes too abstract. I can glean noble characteristics and derive the concept of good, but I cannot love a god of multiple personalities or the concept of goodness.

I once embraced a New Age approach to life. Before long, I did nothing religious or spiritual.

I felt smug with my new solutions to problems that few people take the time to think about, but without a teacher to elucidate the hidden secrets found in the works of the Master DK, as he made little sense to me, I soon realized I stopped like a dead watch, making no spiritual progress at all. Maybe tradition feels a little backward by forcing us to go to church, but that helped make me think about God.

There Is Mortal Sin That Leads to Nonsurvival

This contradicts a beautiful win-win theory. If someone nicks a perfect finish, the brand-new car contains a flaw. Some facts, though hard to accept, turn out true. Do we really want a serial killer or those who force children into pornography or trade women as slaves to return to the earth over and over again? If we loved God so much that we were killed for his sake, do we want to find out that we've got eight more lifetimes? This short and eventful life on earth provides enough evidence for God to know if we are interested in the rest of his universe adventure and want to enroll in his eternal service or not.

New Age Sin

Esoteric studies teach that the only sins in the universe are separateness and cruelty. Separateness finds a home in those who withhold information. A totalitarian regime survives on hiding truth and broadcasting lies. Separateness allows for no concern for others, sometimes eliminating those of a different culture or belief. Some call no man their brother. They are in this struggle alone.

I do not believe in a chosen people. God doesn't favor one son over the other. I do not believe that anyone who does not share my beliefs should be enslaved or exterminated. I should extend goodwill to all. Separateness has no place in religion. The mixing of religion and politics foments danger, especially when the propaganda and training of youth come out of Hitler's handbook.

The practice of cruelty divides goodness from evil. Unfortunately, to stop evil, we often cross the line and engage in cruel acts to not be killed. That epitomizes the tragedy of war: what it does to good men.

Usually we uncover extenuating circumstances. Man fails when attempting a perfect delineation of ethics. Only God judges righteously.

If a violent man commits rape and the woman has an abortion, I would place both sins on the rapist. The woman, making an unethical decision, served as the instrumental but not the primary cause of the abortion. The assailant created this situation. If I were on a jury, I would convict the rapist for both sins and let the woman go free.

We, like the German soldier helping the child into the cattle car, tend to not use the word *crime* to describe our purposely remaining blind to our lack of participation or indifference to murder. We find ways to even excuse cruelty.

Heroes wrestling in the guts of life, many accepting dangerous assignments with the motive of making this a safer and better world, seem to view only very serious offenses as sinful. These transgressions fall under separateness and cruelty.

If these represent the only sins, the whole matter boils down to how I act toward others. I can have a clean slate, not a single check mark on my list of sins—don't covet your neighbor's wife, don't lie, don't swear, go to church, abstain from meat—only to find God works off a different list! What have I done for my fellow man? Do I have a love for the truth? Do I search everywhere and anywhere for righteousness, and did I go myself in search of God? A Christian God would further ask if I know God personally.

I think the New Age identifying separateness and cruelty as the deadly sins of humanity serves as a useful tool that every nation and their leaders should reflect upon.

These form the essence of mortal sin or the death of one's soul, meaning spiritual and final death. Christians say that the soul continues in eternal separation from God and eternal suffering, making God guilty of separateness and cruelty. Theologians explain this as a consequence of divine justice. What does one do with an immortal soul, ever remaining a stand-alone entity, that's bad? New Age believes in survival for all. They would call this bad karma, and the soul would have to reincarnate many times to face some difficult lives ahead to learn its lessons and begin to build up some good karma.

Some of the Christian sins slip through the New Age sieve. Should they be ignored?

Are we better off with or without the Ten Commandments? If every individual followed these, would this be a better world? The church expanded the examination of conscience to cover every sin known to man, including acts of separateness and cruelty. Should we not live a self-examined life?

Since the Ten Commandments improve man's standing before God and man's standing before man as a responsible member of society, we can't go wrong obeying them. A spiritual person sees the spirit of these laws, so he does not follow every law to the letter.

Are There Things We Call Sin, which Are Really the Evolving Mores of a Society?

Are there men working at a "higher level" who can ignore what we call sin?

The commingling of the evolving social mores of society and our evolving religious concepts makes it difficult to separate actual sin from mores that keep society healthy.

The relationship between man and woman evolved into the bond of marriage. Marriage stands as a human achievement, albeit two spirit-led persons have the best chance of making it successful. It ranks as the crowning achievement of a healthy civilization. So making its dissolution a mortal sin may be adding a spiritual millstone to the couple's heartache, but it did help strengthen society from becoming lax and destroying itself through fast marriages and easy divorces.

We even question certain moral lessons ascribed to Jesus and wonder if they were not actually spoken by an apostle and if certain passages got added later to the Gospels.

The apostles could not help but inject their strong opinions against divorce into the Gospels and attribute them to Jesus. Jesus did not spiritually condemn divorce but did refer to a breakdown in Mosaic law to allow this practice. He made it clear that the ideal remains one man and one woman in a lifetime of shared service.

Although esoteric teachings do not view conjugality before or even after marriage with another partner as a sin, they do distinguish whether it was done with love or merely for pleasure.

Esoteric teachings appear to hand out a free card! As long as I act out of love, we conclude there's nothing wrong with sex, and so there is no guilt. Even if done only for sex, I file it away as a lesson to learn. Oh, sure, save it for the next lifetime! I can enjoy unlimited sex and work off any bad karma way later. Sounds good to me!

This helps attract many to the New Age. What adolescent wouldn't buy into this? When I taught in the inner city, young girls informed me there's nothing wrong with making love. In eighth grade, their plan was to have children and go on welfare.

Given the many divorces, being welcomed with a "No problem" nonchalant attitude serves as an appealing invitation.

Marriage blesses humanity with society's greatest human achievement and leads to the founding of a home, the foundation of all social advances. I don't, however, concur mortal sin should be attached to divorce.

The rules around sex and marriage derive more from our evolution and the mores of society than God's commands. That does not mean they can be ignored and anything goes. Killing a society versus killing a soul still does serious harm. Nietzsche wanted elders to approve a marriage and viewed irresponsibly having children as a crime against society.

One-night stands and masturbation suggest selfishness. I'm not sure if this falls under sin or immaturity or both.

Are There Men Working at a "Higher Level" Who Can Ignore Things We Call Sin?

The biographies of men who stand out exude this quality of a "greater love."

We sometimes meet people who have a deep concern for others. They treat friends like a brother. Abraham Lincoln possessed this trait. For a man of major historical significance, historians often point out this overriding quality and say we really should get to know this man of outstanding character. What a wonderful thing to be remembered for.

I had a friend who fought in Vietnam, enjoyed the company (bed) of many women and focused on the heart of important matters and little worried about the rest. He went out of his way to help those in need. He folded up meek before God. He expressed a deep love for Christ, often out loud in conversations.

From my background, he was riddled with mortal sins (missed Mass, engaged in fornication, stood ready to fight with someone who insulted his parents or country, etc.). Yet his relationship with God, his parents, and his friends glowed bright with the fire of love.

I certainly did not care for anyone as deeply as he did. I wondered how he was able to love so much. What I called mortal sins and would be very depressed about, he was taught were natural (sex) or social events (missing church) and did not worry about them.

Hence the idea of a New Age master making major decisions to help mankind and viewing many sins we consider of primary importance to be petty appealed to me. Incidentally, the esoteric astrologer I mentioned earlier identified my friend as a master.

This concept Nietzsche developed. He spoke of an overman doing acts of love that go beyond good and evil. This realm lies above or over man's mere ethics. Kierkegaard also backed this idea as a leap of faith that transforms an ethical and serious religious person into a spiritual man who stands alone before Christ, every moment—a life that only wills the good, to be like Christ in everything, even in suffering.

Jesus explained that he did not wish to abolish the Ten Commandments but fulfill them. He summed them in the positive form that love matters most. Unless our love exceeds that of the Pharisees' obedience to laws, we head toward trouble.

Jesus looks beyond our misguided thinking and bodily desires and sees a soul of great value. We view imperfections as evidence of a soul of little worth.

We must distinguish one feeling above ethics and going beyond ethics.

We cannot take another's life because we feel superior to them.

We can certainly assassinate Hitler after he gassed the first victim.

Love knows all the rules and further understands their intent. Love can honor the spiritual purpose while seemingly breaking the rule.

Spiritual Teachers

I hope to always call this old high school buddy my friend. His life approach to what signifies real sin and what comprises just being human still intrigues me. Such people influence us, many serving as spiritual teachers.

In high school, I found Soren Kierkegaard. He cured me of despair by calling despair sin, and sin starts an avalanche that accumulates as it crashes down into the valley of deep despair. He so influenced me that I went to the seminary and dedicated my career to be the same as his, knowing Christ better.

I never felt a greater calm and deeper love than during my two years studying for the priesthood. But lousy reality crept in. I received one bad grade in the Old Testament (the wonderful priest gave out almost all low grades), which leads to flunking out, which meant going to Vietnam. So to avoid tipping those dominoes, I transferred out and settled into a routine life.

I don't think we realize how much we can influence one another.

Later in life, I went to a men's renewal. I wouldn't think hearing another's journey and daily grind would be interesting. Yet an honest sharing of how someone else tries to keep God alive throughout their challenges and worries, many of which were the same as mine, had an enormous impact. It reminded me to take time for what matters, and I renewed my relationship with Christ. The hand of God may be there on many occasions but materialized as being evident when I looked for spiritual answers. Whatever issue weighed on my mind, I soon found a resource that knew something about it. I encountered a spiritual guide.

I felt anxious about many things in high school and became rather introspective. We were bombarded with world problems, presented as unquestioned and unsolvable. Most of us succumbed to despair.

The first sentence I come across by Kierkegaard states that all men live in despair. Many stay that way to their death. That insight surprised me. He would identify hopeless problems and then find solutions. He changed my thinking and cured me spiritually.

Everything I wanted to know, before long, I ran across in a book or met someone who answered my questions. I didn't always agree with the answer, but it always kept me going and challenged me to keep looking. The promise of Jesus, "Knock, and the door will open, seek, and you will find," proved true.

A friend told me that math seems pointless since it's all been answered. That could apply to most subjects; at least most classes approach the material as "Here's a ton of info I know. Now you need to know." We've forgotten there pop up many questions in every subject that are unanswered and hardly understood. When electricity became known, we made marvelous strides in its use. Yet we still don't know what electricity is; we only know how to measure and make use of it. Another discovery waits.

We should approach all subjects, including religion, recognizing there remains a lot more to discover and learn. The people who suggested the world was round roused more enthusiasm than those who taught the world was square. End of story.

The Spirit of Truth leads us. Always in front, life-giving, enthusiastic, and driving us to keep asking and to uncover. We know how easy we can ignore this Spirit and go about our business. Unfortunately, we're ignoring Jesus, the greatest spiritual teacher.

Living your life in service to others, as advocated by esoteric studies, Jesus did.

God made each one of us a valuable part of God. Like a tapestry, one thread missing will detract from the whole. One colored strand added greatly increases the beauty and brings the work closer to completion.

This perfectly describes God the Supreme, a direct creation and one of the many sons of God the Father. It does not, however, fully describe God the Father.

Esoteric studies contain teachings that are true but concern "lesser gods" or creations of God. It does not reach high enough to know about the Universal God, or God as three Persons. But it can be a stepping stone.

If we glean the sublime personality traits of the masters, we will soon love those persons and see Jesus in them.

I imagine this as God's thinking:

"My sons are all so different and go their separate ways. Some find me in their fellow man, whom they can see. Some turn their backs on me and squander everything, only to realize my house will always be the best and return home. I am your Father. I know you, and my spirit will lead you to me.

"Do not stand self-satisfied. Continue to search for the truth from whatever source keeps you thinking. All truth leads to me.

"I will give you eternal life, and all your questions will be answered."

Conclusion

If you judge a tree by its fruit, there doesn't seem to be much in what goes by the New Age movement.

Everyone's now convinced that Jesus came as a prophet, a good man; someone who can be ignored. We discover lots of self-interest pursuits, new ways of making ourselves better, and no one's gotten any better.

Much of what we've discovered about ourselves to date seems hardly a cause for celebration.

I'd like to see a breakthrough. Can we learn more about a man from esoteric astrology? Can we discern the work of the earth's spiritual hierarchy by the spiritual rays? Can we cure a malady by shining light into a chakra centered in the pituitary gland? Fascinating, but right now, it looks like teachings offering little help.

14

The Rebirth of Christians

Spark

I like the analogy of a spark to describe a spirit, a part of God.

God the Father places a spark in our mind.

We provide kindling. Jesus's breath ignites it, and a fire spreads. This happened at Pentecost.

If we keep covering the spark with mud, it extinguishes. We find a lot of mud on earth.

If taught wilderness survival, we find it amazing how quickly we create a blazing campfire from one tiny spark. If far away and freezing, this skill becomes critical. Our survival depends on knowing what gets a fire going and what puts it out.

How much of Christ shows in what I am doing? Jesus's acid test here on earth consisted of asking whether a situation brought him closer to God or farther away.

If every child from Jesus's time knew God as their Father and everything else fell secondary, would the world be significantly different from today? I don't know.

But I know fire makes the difference. Some hearts are burning, and their lives encircle Christ. These people change the world for the better.

What distinguishes the apostles, Soren Kierkegaard, Martin Luther, and others boils down to a strong relationship with Christ. They may be theologically flawed and have done or said wrong things, but their hearts were burning to know Christ more deeply, and they tried every day to strengthen their relationship with him. The overriding impetus of their life became Christ. That made all the difference.

Relationships survive death. Not much else does and simply serves as scaffolding.

We cannot make love grow. By experience, we learn to love. We don't provide the fire; we can only bring kindling. We must provide fuel if we want the fire to stay alive and grow.

I still find life a grueling struggle with only faint glimpses of hope. It never seems easy. I may never be someone where the love flows; I don't recall seeing many like that in my life. But that's the goal. Through daily experience, we're getting wiser and discerning where to find the better fuel. I hope I get called home while warming my hands before a blaze.

Future

I keep forgetting we haven't gotten very far from standing upright. I'm impatient for mankind to make some dramatic change, but that resembles more the way of Lucifer. We plod along at a slow pace. I don't expect much change, other than a more devastating war and more human suffering.

When we fought the costly Civil War, we pitted brother against brother, with either the sovereignty of each Southern state or the Union foremost in soldiers' minds.

Because we shared one language, we shared a greater realization that we were fighting brother against brother.

Because we shared one spiritual foundation—being a Christian—we shared a willingness to fight for what we considered a just cause, and each desired to live together in peace.

When the war ended, every state gave up their sovereignty and we became one nation. We established a single government for the good of all, with each state represented regardless of size.

The same will happen with the world. Too soon, and it will be a totalitarian regime like in *1984*. In the far future, a democratic, sovereign, and service-to-all-men government, with each country having equal representation regardless of size, will happen if the following take place:

- If we speak one language. When men speak different languages, there cultivates a lack of trust.

- If we center ourselves in Christ. Unless we become more spiritual, nothing good will happen.

  The only up-stepping of mankind today can be by spiritual means. An individual first seeks the kingdom of heaven and then improves other areas he touches. The Gospels imply that we will see Christ returning to earth with our spiritual eyes. If he visits tomorrow, we would not see him.

I know other religions find it offensive that without Jesus Christ they are left out. Certainly, without the values of Jesus, they are out. If they love a god that has the love and character of Jesus, under another name, then "a rose by any other name would still smell as sweet." If they turn their back on such a person, they turn their back on Christ. They choose out.

• If we willingly surrender our national sovereignty for the good of all on this planet. To find altruistic leaders who view a position of world power as a heavy responsibility and are willing to serve all men seems a long way off.

Many states were burned to the ground before surrendering their sovereignty during the Civil War. Causalities were extreme, and families lost everything. All this is coming. I state this not as prophecy but an extrapolation of trends. Only the Spirit of Truth, the living spirit of Jesus, curbs the aggressive nature in each of us. If we find no peace in us, there follows a lack of peace in our families, and this aggressiveness often breaks out into war. Conflicts become more devastating as technology advances.

So what's all this got to do with my raise? The circle of our concerns extends sadly limited, like a hollow dot.

One poet described Christmas as the time when we widen our circle.

We don't know what God has planned for us. The birth of his Son, Jesus, gave great light to our backward planet. God remains still very much in control. Thank God.

Unity

Jesus did not desire uniformity. He saw faith as one's personal journey.

Every relationship forms uniquely. We each have our own personality and mind, and the spirit within approaches each in a way that guarantees the greatest benefit. We were meant to question and search and explore and read and reread and then search some more for deeper truth. Life hardly consists of a course for dummies, where we memorize a book with answers and then repeat them our whole life. That can be the downside of belonging to an established church. We are to partner with Jesus and let his Spirit of Truth lead us anywhere that brings us closer to truth. That way, we experience truth for ourselves, partner with the God dwelling in our minds, and form roots that drive down deep into Jesus, the good soil.

Jesus did demand unity.

Each church denomination became a castle with a theological hatchet man chopping heads off dissenters. Anxious dwellers just sign the papers, figuring that in this castle I was born, and in here I wish to die. Besides, castles have experts who figure all this stuff out without me having to do anything. Call it a bene. To play it safe, don't question doctrines or ask yourself what you believe.

If the primary message of Jesus attests that we are sons and daughters of God, all that would matter would be forming a deep love for Christ from our personal encounters with him, and then this includes all that Jesus wanted us to know. All Christians have this foundation. All men of goodwill can begin here. We stand united in our starting position.

If the message St. Paul spread throughout the world contained the key teaching from Jesus—that we are sons and daughters of God—we might be enjoying the fruits of a single, unified Christlike faith.

It grows critical that Christians unite. Anti-Christian forces continue on the move, usurping higher ground. We will lose if we do not unite. We deem Christ worth saving on this earth.

Conclusion

What, as a Christian, should I do?

1. Know the faith, as taught by Jesus.
    Our Christian faith reveals the truth that we have one Father, God.
    Then we are sons and daughters of God.
    That makes us brothers and sisters.

    In a good and loving family,

    *   children emulate their parents;

- children are watched over, cared for, and loved by parents;

- children are unquestionably part of a family;

- children are immature and make mistakes, parents understand, and children reconcile quickly and get back to the way things were;

- children don't worry;

- children want to please their parents;

- children are happy, innocent, and only know love;

- children want their parents around 24-7 and love to talk to them;

- children know the rules and don't break them; and

- children don't play with bad kids.

Of all the ways, especially for someone sovereign, God chose to come to earth as a baby, one of a family: Jesus, with Mary and Joseph. He continued to extend his family. He lived with his apostles as a family. He taught them that all men are their brothers and sisters; all men belong to God's family.

We humans are sons and daughters of God the Father. Jesus called this his good news.

If your master whom you love ends up getting tortured and killed and then resurrects himself, it's easy to see how the lesson Jesus taught would be exchanged for the thrilling fact that everything Jesus said—that he was God—and all his promises about everlasting life turned out true.

It seems unthinkable that a Father with unlimited powers would allow his Son to die an ignominious and torturous death, like one we could face.

Jesus did not come as a sacrifice, as if the murder of a son could have any meaning other than heartbreak.

Jesus intended to perform no miracles. For one with unlimited powers, this decision reveals the nature of God. Even when finding himself in a horrible and unjust situation, he did not resort to his authority, not even to his human advantage of eloquent speech or an iron-clad intellectual defense. "He cast no pearls." His life and his teachings were one and the same.

2. Strengthen the church.

Christians are, and always have been, a light to a dark world.

All of them folks who wanted to kill Jesus back then did not go away. They just improved their methods. We have not dug out of the deep snow from the continuous blizzard of anti-Christian sentiment and slander. Wherever we see melted snow, we see the work of Christ.

I discovered a few new books on the Crusades where historians admit that prior accounts were seriously tainted by anti-Christian sentiment. The accepted belief that both sides were aggressors vying for land becomes clarified that the Christians were either defending their land or taking back what was stolen from them. The accepted belief that Christians, due to their greed, joined the Crusades to make a fortune gave way to finding out these men left family and home for their beliefs, many leaving their families destitute.

Many good works in serving Jesus go unrecognized. I never even heard of the Knights of Columbus until I aged into my late fifties. It stands out as a national organization of Catholic men who do an enormous amount of charitable works. The Salvation Army stays centered in Christ but are known only for their bell ringing. We rarely find either mentioned in any paper. Yet they make this world better.

Don't downplay Jesus.

When we suggest that the faith of Jesus is more important than a faith in Jesus, we emphasize how Christians act. Truth keeps paces ahead like some fitness trainer. This makes us get off the couch, do ten jumping jacks, and run after him! Jesus went about doing good works.

The more we learn about Jesus, the more we love him. The more we love him, the more we act like him.

We center on Jesus when we reflect, "*Jesus* would want us to do this. Remember when *Jesus* spoke to that troubled youth? What did he say? How pleasing this work must be to *our* Father."

We need to make it clear that we do all these things because Jesus did these same things. We don't stoop and pretend that Jesus cannot be present or be God because we are open-minded and want to be accepted by more religions. That would be like a rich man feigning poverty at a fund-raiser.

Support and love for fellow Christians goes a long way. Simple encouragement uplifts our spirits. We are called to lift each load together. Our spiritual leaders should be applauded and financially enabled to do their good works.

Everyone who wants Jesus's attention receives it. He changes lives by his gracious words of encouragement and hope. When kids interrupt his discussions, he makes them the center of attention. How children love to hear Jesus tell them stories! All we do, we do because we want to do what Jesus did. And Jesus did the will of his Father, who is also our Father.

The Trinity presents a profound revelation that only Christians know. This discloses a truth God wants all to know. Like a solid first step in a proof, if we start here, the rest follows. Without it, error ensues. How could God be a father without a son? How can they love without a spirit of love?

Since half of God's creation falls under female, I infer that the feminine traits reside with God and manifest in the Holy Spirit.

The all-important love between a parent and their children comes perfectly instantiated between God the Father and God the Son. It took us a million years to evolve enough to draw up a marriage contract with one partner. We earned our highest evolutionary achievement, marriage and family. We emulate God because God is a family and has a family.

Evolution only takes us so far.

Evolution makes a more developed man. Experience makes a better man. God makes us a spiritual man. As Kierkegaard observed, man advances from aesthetic to ethical/religious to spiritual. If we desire to know God, we advance.

The church brings together individuals who wish to know God and leads them in the public worship of God.

The church is not Christ. We base a church's value on how much of Christ it contains. Jesus preferred to worship in beautiful outdoor settings. He understands that men want to worship together and fosters the church.

The question never goes away: "Why do I have to go to church?" Another question follows: "What will we replace it with?" I had sound arguments, and sure I'd become a better person.

I enjoyed my freedom of where and when to worship. Before long, I did nothing. I spiritually stagnated.

Even if we've found some better way and commune with God throughout the day, we should go to church. Help others. Support others. Learn from others. Cooperative teams invariably provide the better solution. Ten can easily lift what one cannot.

Christians can no longer afford to be a house divided. The American Indians did not unite to form a nation until it was too late.

My brother and sister and I agree and disagree on many subjects. What matters boils down to we are one family. We are individuals, each with our own personality and unique mind. Our family gives us unity, not uniformity.

Christians know of one God in three persons, the Trinity. Christians know God as a father. Christians love Jesus as his divine Son. Most everything else ends up in a theological war. Would we rather stand at judgment and proclaim we can recite every law of the church, or that our heart burned when we learned something new about Jesus? That we believe transubstantiation or that we many times feel the personal presence of Jesus?

We must supply the conditions for growth. God will gladly take care of the rest.

Let's pick our battles carefully. Christians must unite.

All glory goes to God. Religious leaders are not God, and possess no divine powers. Nothing that any of us do would have any meaning without God.

3. Know thyself.

The only solution to man is God. We are an animal, with a fragment of God that dwells within. That explains why man acts like an animal; that explains why man acts like a son of God.

There exists a fragment of God the Father that dwells in all normal men and women's minds. Jesus said the kingdom of God lives within. Kierkegaard referred to this entity as the "self." This enables us a divine part, our thought adjuster, currently on loan.

A wise human forms a partnership with something divine within and vastly superior. The thought adjuster creates the immortal part of our soul, placing diamonds with an attached transcription of each good thing we do. This comprises the immortal part of our soul. But that doesn't make us immortal.

We have free will. We can be presented with the most beautiful gifts and refuse them all. The spirit world will never force any man. At death, the thought adjuster takes the diamonds, and we cease to exist if we showed no interest. Or we desire to make the partnership permanent, and those diamonds become ours forever. When we fuse with our thought adjuster, then our soul—we—become immortal, and we live forever.

Where do I plan to be a million years from now? We should begin working on our short-term goals today!

Christians live forever.

Kierkegaard was right. He lived his life totally dependent on God. The close relationship God offers us amazed him, and he concentrated on that relationship daily. Every word of Jesus he meditated on and took to heart. He gave up all for the one he loved, Jesus.

Nietzsche was right. What we call Christianity hardly resembles what Jesus taught and acted upon. What we call Christianity often turns out its opposite. Christians defend the dissolute.

We form church tribes, fight with bows and arrows against rifles, and refuse to unite on any ground including being eradicated. Our tolerance of evil hardly ranks us among the spiritually strong. We seem unaware of the sinful willingly, and the good unwittingly carrying out the advice of Caligastia, Lucifer's representative on earth.

We will not defeat Caligastia by making excuses, offering our psychological understanding, or hoping for a last minute confession. He willingly moved beyond that. Caligastia will not be exterminated until *we* give up all sympathy toward him.

Jesus was right. Jesus taught son-ship with God, the greatest truth ever revealed. Remember how when we were a kid, it was such a great feeling just to be alive. That's how Jesus approached life. As a father, remember how we solve an issue that our son or daughter caused, and we grew to love each other more after we settled it. That's how our Heavenly Father helps us. That's why Jesus became so enthused when talking about his Father.

I did not solve the world's problems. I sense no surprise. I do know step one remains to seek first the kingdom of heaven—we all have one Father, God, making us sons and daughters of God. That's all we know and all we need to know. Live as a son of God.

Form does not change hearts. Theology does not change hearts. Meeting Jesus changes hearts. A person who formulates relationships by theology bears little love. Our jobs, all the knowledge we need to stay employed, even our theology, we put aside when our children run to greet us. Our Heavenly Father does the same.

Truth must pass this simple test: if it's something we would allow for our sons and daughters, we can count on our Heavenly Father's approval of the same, only more far sighted and loving.

One hurdle we face centers on God being invisible. Spirit reigns superior to matter and unseen by human eyes. Someday we will be invisible too. That doesn't mean we won't exist. Why do we tolerate such nonsense as concluding that God does not exist?

We hear this often from many at the top. Do you think a vastly intelligent spirit, one who studied man's thinking for billions of years, won't go after someone with power, influence, and authority? Especially since these gifted people often don't believe in God, an afterlife, or anything invisible. Selling their soul for more earthy gains, hubris, and unfair advantages offers easy pickings and key wins, with dire consequences to Christians. Caligastia wants humans to influence and destroy other humans. He's quite the executive. He helps spread the belief that rebellious beings of a higher order (such as him) do not exist. Ignorance equals vulnerability to deception and manipulation.

We must defeat Caligastia and lose all sympathy for him and his horrible plans on earth. We must be wise as serpents. May the peace of Jesus disturb us.

To Rick & Donna,

This should Challenge your
bible studies! Greatly enjoyed
your sons - what better credential
than Christian children.

Gregg D. Jonesko